You're a Miracle!

My Story of Alcoholism, Miraculous Healing, and God's Infinite Power and Love

by Joe McGivney

You're a Miracle

My Story of Alcoholism, Miraculous Healing, and God's Infinite Power and Love

You're a Miracle is a work of nonfiction. To protect their privacy, the names of some individuals, places, and institutions may have been changed.

This book contains general information about addiction, recovery, and related matters. The information is not medical advice. This book is not an alternative to medical advice from your doctor or other professional healthcare provider.

ISBN: 979-8-9889389-0-3

SURRENDER PUBLISHING LLC

To my darling wife Nicole. Thank you for being my angel, the heart of our family, and the Joy of My Life. I love you!

To my children Ally and Colin. Thank you teaching me the true meaning of forgiveness and unconditional love. I love you!

To my brothers and sisters in recovery. May you stand in the Presence of Infinite Power and Love.

Foreword

By Scott A. O'Connor
Supreme Director, Knights of Columbus

You're a Miracle provides an insight into one man's journey of addiction, his total submission to the destructive power of alcohol, and how it cost him everything, including his wife and nearly his life, but it does not end there….

This story of the life of Joe McGivney is a story about miracles and how Joe, who is believed to be a relative of Blessed Michael J. McGivney, founder of the Knights of Columbus, through the power of Prayer and the Holy Spirit, got back all he had lost and more.

Joe tells us about a life spent in years of alcohol abuse, and how on December 30, 2020, it all came crashing in on him when his body no longer could cope. Joe's wife Nicole would get him to the Jupiter Medical Center (Florida) where Joe became more and more noncompliant and even dangerous. Joe tells us how he was "frequently restrained, straps on my wrists and ankles, a roll belt around my waist." He was transferred to several different medical facilities over a three-month period, including St. Mary's Medical Center where they diagnosed his condition as Wernicke-Korsakoff Syndrome (WKS), a condition often referred to as "Wet Brain." Joe's condition had progressed to full-blown Korsakoff Psychosis, the extreme form of WKS, which includes hallucinations and severe amnesia. Most patients of WKS need 24/7 care for the condition that typically would be unchanging for the remainder of their lives.

But Joe would not be one of those patients, in fact, Joe would become a Miracle, for on March 6, 2021, he woke up and was completely well. Joe tells us about a conversation with his Aunt Gerry, a McGivney relative, a nurse and family member who had kept in touch with Nicole during Joe's sickness and had been an encouraging voice. Aunt Gerry was the first person to let Joe know that his recovery was unique. The next person to do so, a psychiatrist, informed Joe, "Do you know that you're a miracle?" The psychiatrist proceeded to tell Joe about other patients she had treated over the years and stated that "they don't recover like you have, and certainly not completely and overnight." Joe received other similar comments from doctors and medical personnel, all stating that his recovery was nothing short of remarkable. It was around that time, during one of Joe's conversations with his Aunt Gerry, that she informed him of the prayer chain she had led with the McGivney family, praying for Blessed Michael McGivney's intercession, "for him to intercede for you to God. And he did." Joe tells the reader of the fireworks that were going off inside his head when he realized that "The love of God had intervened in my life and done something for me that only he could do. He himself had reached down and touched me and drawn me back from destruction."

Joe's story continues as he shares how he returned to the faith, to the Holy Roman Catholic Church, how he and Nicole were reunited and married again, how Nicole, moved by being witness to the power of the Holy Spirit at work, became Catholic.

Joe's story has been featured in several publications including the internationally distributed Columbia

Magazine. Joe is a frequent speaker at Knights of Columbus events and was the Keynote Speaker at the 2021 Florida State Convention of the Knights of Columbus. Joe's story has even been submitted and accepted for review by the McGivney Guild, an organization that oversees review of submitted "favors" of Blessed Michael McGivney's intercession. The Guild upon conducting its research can submit the "favor" for consideration by the Vatican for a 2nd Miracle attributed to Blessed Michael McGivney's intercession, needed for his Canonization.

I highly recommend this book for anyone who has ever struggled with or known someone who has struggled with substance abuse. The book provides a rare insight into the power of prayer and the fact that miracles do happen in our modern world. I have known Joe and his family for several years and am convinced that he is living proof that anything is possible with God. Joe continues his work with the Knights of Columbus, proclaiming the Good News and practicing the virtues of Charity, Unity, and Fraternity in his daily life.

CONTENTS

Chapter 1: "Wet Brain"

I surrender to you my whole self, my heart, my mind, my memory. – the SURRENDER PRAYER

On December 30, 2020, I lost my mind. Literally. After another long day of drinking, I suddenly collapsed on the living room floor in our home in an upscale gated community of Palm Beach Gardens, Florida. It would be nine weeks before I had another coherent thought.

I would end up losing my mind to such a degree that I would be "Baker-Acted" by the end of those nine weeks. The Baker Act is the Florida Mental Health Act that allows for the involuntary institutionalization of an individual. In other words, I was so far gone that a court ruled I was no longer capable of making my own decisions.

And I wasn't. In fact, I remember nothing from those nine weeks, except for some deeply ingrained hallucinations. Everything I will share with you about that period I learned later from others and from medical records. *I* remember nothing about those nine weeks, but they were filled with pain, darkness, sadness, and fear for my wife and family.

I must have had my cell phone near me when I fell on the living room floor that night because I somehow managed to call my wife, who had already gone upstairs to bed. "Nicole," I said, "something's really wrong. Please come help me."

1

She came down to find me fumbling for words, confused, and hardly able to stand on my feet. One way or another, she got me into her SUV. She tells me I was leaning against her as we walked to the vehicle. My wife is five-foot, ninety-pounds soaking wet, as pretty as she is petite, and at the time I was an alcohol-bloated 220 pounds. I don't know how she did it to this day.

She got me in the vehicle and headed for the nearest hospital, Jupiter Medical Center. She was worried, of course, that I was having a stroke, one of the banes of the alcoholic. I had had a few early warning signs. I was experiencing vision, balance, and memory issues, which no doctor could seem to explain.

I had been a heavy drinker for many years, but during COVID I took it to another level. It was not only the extra time I had on my hands, but my worries about my financial situation. The company I worked for—I am a financial advisor—closed every office. My income dropped dramatically, and I didn't know if my role in the industry would ever come back. Would I be able to keep a roof over our heads? Would I be able to educate my children? Those fears spiraled out of control, and my solution was to medicate with alcohol.

I have to smile a little bit when I think about how crazy my daily drinking regime had become during COVID. About 7:00 a.m. Nicole would leave for work. She's a teacher at a private school, and her school did not shut down for COVID. At 7:10 a.m. I would hop in my car—giving her that 10-minute head start so we wouldn't end up at the same stoplight. I would then drive to a liquor store that opened at 7:00 a.m., pull in, buy exactly three mini-bottles of vodka, and drink them right there in the parking lot. There was a reason why I did this. It was really important for me to be able to jump in the car and drive in case of an emergency, so I knew I had to keep my blood alcohol level below 0.08. I had a breathalyzer at home and had learned that three shots of vodka would put me right at a 0.075 blood alcohol level, right below the legal limit. I had also learned that it took each shot exactly one hour to leave my body, so at 9:15 a.m. I could drive back to the liquor store and do two more shots, at 11:15 a.m. drive back and do another two, and the same thing at 1:15 p.m. and 3:15 p.m.

One time the clerk at the liquor store said, "Rather than come back here and just buy two little bottles at a time, why don't you just buy a big one? It'll be cheaper, and it'll save you gas."

"Trust me," I said, "There's a method to my madness." The reason was this: I knew that if I bought that big bottle, I would drink the whole thing. Buying a couple little bottles at a time was a way of self-regulating.

By 5:15 p.m. Nicole was home from work, and I no longer had to worry about being ready to drive. About the only things open during COVID were grocery stores and liquor stores. She would drive us to the grocery store to figure out what to eat that night, and on the way out I'd stop in the liquor store right next door, do three more shots, and buy a bottle or two of wine to get me through the night. I did all of this *every single day* from early March 2020 until December 30, 2020—when my mind and body finally gave out and put me on my living room floor.

Nicole got me to Jupiter Medical Center. They met her at the emergency room entrance, put me in a wheelchair, and took me away. Nicole wasn't allowed to go in with me because of the COVID protocols. In all likelihood, Nicole saved my life that night. Just a few months later, she would save my life again.

So began my institutional odyssey: During that nine-week period, I would pass through some eight separate facilities, including hospitals, rehabs, treatment centers, and nursing homes, as doctors tried to figure out what was wrong with me and staff tried to figure out how to handle me. I was a noncompliant patient at best and at worst a dangerous one. I was frequently restrained, straps on my wrists and ankles, a roll belt around my waist. When I wasn't being defiant, I was being downright looney. I was hallucinating that my feet were monsters or that imaginary people were in the room with me or that I was playing board games with my children. One time I stripped down to walk naked through the halls, moaning, "I want a beer," knocking on other patients' doors, or just busting in and scaring them. I was finally deposited in the psychiatric ward at St. Mary's Medical Center, a *locked* psych ward.

It was at St. Mary's that they eventually diagnosed my condition. I had Wernicke-Korsakoff Syndrome (WKS), a serious and dangerous neurological disorder also known as "Wet Brain" because of its prevalence among alcoholics. It is triggered by a severe deficiency of vitamin B1, or thiamine, an essential nutrient for brain function. Alcohol impedes the digestive tract's ability to absorb and process thiamine, thus triggering the disorder.

However, I had "progressed" to full-blown Korsakoff Psychosis, the extreme form of WKS, which includes hallucinations and severe amnesia. In

Korsakoff Psychosis, the brain has been rewired in such a way that it no longer has the ability to form new memories. It's common for these patients to have full recall of the first 20 or 30 years of their lives and then everything ends. They're stuck in a world where they can't remember what they did five minutes ago let alone a day, week, or month ago, a perpetual *Groundhog Day* that never ends. That is the world I was now living in, and that is how I was supposed to be for the rest of my life. There is no cure for someone who has progressed to the extreme that I had.

The day came when the doctors told Nicole, "He's going to be like this for the rest of his life, needing care 24/7. You have to find a long-term care facility for him." My family was just devastated, and the burden on Nicole was incredible.

But Nicole could find no place to take me. I had run out of options by that time. The only place gracious enough to help at all was the Retreat at Palm Beach, a substance abuse and behavioral health facility. But they stipulated, "Only for 30 days, to give you time to find a permanent solution."

So on March 5, 2021, I was transferred from the locked psych ward at St. Mary's to the Retreat at Palm Beach and put to bed....

The next morning, March 6, 2021, I woke up—and I was *completely well!*

I sat up in the bed, put my feet on the floor, and looked around the simple room—just the bed, a nightstand, a dresser, and a sunny window—and I realized I had no idea where I was.

I stood up. I was wearing a Notre Dame sweatshirt

and a pair of jeans, very baggy jeans because I had lost 60 pounds since my collapse. I went to the door, opened it, and stepped into a hall lined with similar doors. I sort of moseyed along until I found a young staff member and asked him, "What's going on? Where am I?"

He gave me a curious look. "You're at a treatment facility called the Retreat."

"How did I get here?"

"They brought you over from St. Mary's yesterday."

"Why am I here?"

"Because of your drinking."

I saw Nicole the next day. She was blown away to find me sitting there calmly, smiling at her, and chatting pleasantly just like the old days. She burst out, "Joe, what's happening? Just the other day you didn't know who I was! You asked for documentation to prove I was your wife. You thought I was the Uber driver coming to take you to the airport. Now you're perfectly normal! What has happened?"

"I don't know."

In fact, no one knew. In the coming days, I would visit a long string of doctors who could give no explanation for what happened to me. When I went to see my primary care physician after my release from the Retreat, her lips formed a perfect O as I walked into her office as normal as could be. She has treated other Wet Brain patients and fully expected me to be, at best, in a wheelchair pushed by an aide. She gave me a puzzled look and said, "How do you feel?"

"I feel awesome," I answered. "Fantastic."

"I want you to get a full blood workup in the lab and come back and see me in two weeks," she said.

So I did, and this time when I entered her office, she said, "I want to show you something." First, she pulled up my liver enzymes chart from my drinking days and said, "Do you remember this? I told you that a normal liver enzyme reading was between 1 and 35. Anything above that and you're doing permanent damage to your liver."

I nodded. "You said mine was the highest enzyme reading you'd ever seen, 209."

"Your blood work results just came in." She pulled up my new chart and showed it to me. "Your new enzyme reading is 18. In the middle of the normal range."

"Wow," I said. "How is that possible?"

"I don't have an answer for you."

"How do you explain it?" I asked.

She shook her head and said, "There is no explanation."

She was right to a degree. There was no *medical* explanation. But in the days to come I would discover another, more exciting kind of explanation for my spontaneous healing.

Chapter 2: How It Was

I surrender every situation in my life to you. – the SURRENDER PRAYER

Cradle Catholic

Iwas born in June of 1963 at Little Company of Mary Hospital in Evergreen Park, Illinois, a small suburb that borders the Chicago city limits. Everyone I know, every one of my family members, was born at Little Company of Mary, a Catholic hospital run by the nuns. I was the oldest of three children. My sisters were Erin and Shannon. As you can tell by the names, we were Irish, and the neighborhood that we were raised in was predominantly Irish Catholic. Everybody I knew was Catholic, with very few exceptions. The neighborhood where we lived bordered the southwest corner of Chicago, and we very proudly referred to ourselves as Southside Irish.

My parents married in their early 20s. They had been high school sweethearts. In good Irish Catholic tradition, once they married they wanted to start a family, and I was born less than one year after their wedding date. My father was in the insurance and investment industry. My mother was a registered nurse. My childhood could not have been more wonderful. Both of my parents were loving, supportive, kind, and encouraging. It truly was an idyllic childhood.

Our Catholic roots went deep. Ten days after I was

born, I was baptized at St. Margaret of Scotland Catholic Church, which is located on the south side of Chicago. In my early childhood, my family moved to another small suburb on the outskirts of Chicago, Oak Lawn, where we faithfully attended St. Catherine of Alexandria Catholic Church. I made my first Holy Communion at age eight, and I was confirmed at age eleven. Some people are astonished when they hear that I took the sacraments at such a young age, but that's just how it was done in the Chicago Archdiocese.

I attended public school through eighth grade at Kolmar Elementary. I then moved on to Brother Rice High School, an all-boys Catholic prep school. It was an excellent education and kept me close to my Catholic faith. Sadly, the minute I finished at Brother Rice and no longer *had* to go to Mass, I stopped going. Somehow, and through no one's fault but my own, I never made that Divine connection that would keep me tethered to the church. I knew the words, I knew the prayers, but I was just going through the motions. It never became personal. When I went off to college and had the freedom to choose, my Catholic faith was no longer a priority for me. I drifted away from the church.

A Budding Romance

My love affair with alcohol began the summer before 8th grade. I'll never forget the night. It was summertime, it was warm, and we were hanging out in my friend's front yard. My friend's older brother came outside with his keys in his hand, on his way to the liquor store. "Will you buy us some beer?" we asked him.

"You got the money?" he asked.

"Yes!"

He shrugged. "Sure, why not?"

He came back with three six-packs of Old Style. There were six of us boys, so that meant three cans for each of us! I pulled the tab on that first can of beer, heard that refreshing *pop* and *hiss*, and took that first drink—and wanted to vomit! It was awful. But I fought it down—I wanted to be one of the guys—and before I knew it I was *loving* how it made me feel. Like I really fit in.

Even as a boy, I had often felt "less than." My grades were good enough, but I wasn't the smartest kid in class. I was a good athlete, but I wasn't the best. I did okay with the girls, but they weren't throwing themselves at my feet. I always felt a little "less than," a step outside the circle. But all that washed away with my first beer. I belonged. I was one of the guys. I felt confident. I thought I was funny. I just loved how it made me feel. My anxieties drifted away.

From that point on through high school, drinking became a part of my life. I was a "weekend warrior," dry Monday through Thursday, but come the weekend my friends and I would be hanging around outside the liquor store convincing somebody old enough (or with a good fake ID) to buy us beer, wine, or peppermint schnapps. Sometimes we found an excuse to drink during the week as well. Come the weekend, there was always a party somewhere, and I had a long list of drinking buddies.

None of this was unusual in my Irish Catholic world. We celebrated everything—baptisms, first communions, weddings, funerals—and alcohol played a role in all those celebrations. It was just part of who we were. In my own family tree, there were alcoholics hanging from a number of the branches. My parents, thankfully, were an exception.

My drinking continued at the University of Illinois. I was named social chairman of the fraternity I joined, a fancy way of saying I was the guy responsible for ordering beer for all the parties. It's safe to say that I drank every single day of my college career. Not that I was falling-down drunk—I wasn't; I managed to keep my grades up—but whether it was a beer with a friend in my room or several vodka and tonics at the local bar, booze was always present.

I left college early to work in the investment industry at my dad's firm. Here I was, a young man rubbing elbows with grown-ups, men with mortgages, with children, with bills. I admired them and wanted to be like them. They worked hard, and they played hard. It was common to finish a long day at the bar. I didn't have any thought that I had a drinking problem at this time. I was just having fun, celebrating after a productive day. This was my model for what grown-ups did. I realize now that my alcoholism was stealthily progressing all this time, gaining a little more control every day.

The 1987 stock market crash rocked my dad's firm, which ultimately dissolved. I bounced around a bit until I found a role in the investment industry that I would hold for the better part of 30 years. The typical financial advisor works with individuals and families and small business owners, investing their money for them in mutual funds, bonds, etc. My clients, on the other hand, were those financial advisors themselves. My job was to sell them the mutual funds they in turn

11

sold their clients. It paid well, and a big part of the job was entertaining clients—happy hours, dinners at Ruth's Chris, rounds of golf, concerts, sporting events—all on a corporate credit card. I had found my dream job.

In my late 20s and early 30s, I was living in downtown Chicago. I had a large group of interesting and colorful friends. We were all from different places, backgrounds, and had different careers (or lack thereof). We took full advantage of Chicago's vibrant party scene. And we all had one thing in common. We loved to drink.

My First Wife

I met my first wife, the mother of my two wonderful children, Ally and Colin, in my early thirties. We were in love when we got married, but my work often required me to travel three, four days at a time, while she stayed at home taking care of very small children, and in too-typical fashion we drifted apart.

My alcoholism with its attendant selfishness was no doubt a part of it. I was the easiest guy in the world to get along with *as long as* everyone and everything behaved as I wished. But when they didn't, I had something to say about that. The need to be controlling is another trait of the alcoholic.

We moved to South Florida in 2004. My firm offered me the chance to relocate and build up the business in this lucrative region. We thought the move might give us a fresh start. However, the beautiful home, the new boat, and the nice cars could not keep us together. Our problems moved with us. We argued about everything. *Everything.* When we saw the pain

12

our constant bickering and animosity was causing our young children, we decided to divorce—and not very amicably. I know it was very hard on the children. Somehow, by the grace of God, they both turned out to be amazing, wonderful young people.

My True Love

I met Nicole, the true love of my life, in 2008. We met very casually—our first conversation was in a restaurant parking lot—but we immediately hit it off. To me, she was the whole package: not only beautiful, but smart, positive, and never had a bad word to say about anyone. To this day, she is one of the kindest people I have ever known. Somehow she was attracted to me too, finding me chivalrous and mature compared to younger men she had dated. We married in 2010, and I discovered that she was not only a wonderful spouse but a world-class stepmom, immediately becoming a hugely positive influence on my children Ally and Colin. She made a great difference in their education as well. Nicole works at a prestigious private school in Palm Beach, and the school agreed to honor the faculty tuition discount for my children. Ally and Colin were able to attend a private school with a phenomenal academic program.

My chivalrous ways, however, eroded with the growth of my alcoholism. I wasn't yet drinking all day long, but nights and weekends I often overdid it. I would say stupid, hurtful things. During that period, I was starting to have blackout episodes where I would wake up in the morning unsure of how Nicole and I had left things the night before. I'd wake up on the couch with an incredible sense of shame, thinking, *Oh, my*

God. What did I say or do last night? By 2016, Nicole had had enough, and we got divorced.

Within three months, however, we were dating again! We truly loved each other deeply, and this time I promised to work on my drinking. We even went to see a therapist about it, and we reached an agreement. I would not stop drinking, but I would stop binge drinking. Our second wedding was in July of 2019, and for the most part, at least 95 percent of the time, I kept that agreement, because I didn't want to lose Nicole again. I drank daily, but I went to bed and woke up the next morning with a full recall of everything that happened the night before.

The situation was far from perfect, but we were getting by—then COVID hit.

COVID

Come early March 2020, as I detailed in the first chapter, my drinking spiraled out of control. The extra time on my hands, my financial worries and fears, and, frankly, the progression of my disease—it all combined to drive me to "medicate" with alcohol every waking hour. I have calculated how much vodka I was drinking per day with my bi-hourly regime of "mini-shots." It was the equivalent of a full-sized bottle of 80 proof vodka every single day. Not to mention the bottle or two of wine I had each night.

I actually had some warning signs that something bad was coming. I would be sitting on the couch watching TV with Nicole and all of a sudden have double vision, sometimes for a few minutes, sometimes for hours. It was scary. Or we would go to the beach for a walk but within five minutes I had to stop. My legs

14

wouldn't move without a Herculean effort, without a conscious thought on my part forcing them to, and my balance was shaky. I would have to turn to Nicole and say, "Honey, I can't do this. Let's go home."

I went and saw a neuro-ophthalmologist about the double vision. Not a "mere" ophthalmologist but a neurologist too. After a comprehensive exam, this Ivy League-educated specialist failed to consider that I might be in the early stages of Wernicke-Korsakoff Syndrome, though inexplicable vision problems are a flashing red sign of the disease. "I think it's basically just aging, Mr. McGivney," he said. "The muscles in your eyes may be weakening. If it doesn't clear up, let's do some surgery." I hold nothing against him. If he had correctly identified the disorder and advised me to stop drinking, I probably would have ignored his advice anyway.

The amazing thing is, even at this point I would have denied that I had a serious drinking problem, one that I couldn't handle on my own. That's the deceptive power of alcoholism, the disease that convinces its victim that he has no disease. It is, as I would later read in the Big Book of Alcoholics Anonymous, "cunning, baffling, powerful!"

In August 2020, it became time to take my daughter to college for her freshman year. By the end of that trip, I would no longer be able to deny my problem. She had been admitted to Florida State University in Tallahassee, and we had rented an apartment there for her. So we packed her up and headed north on the Florida Turnpike for the six-hour drive. Nicole and I had agreed to split the driving. I don't know how I pulled it off, but the night before, I managed not to drink so that I could keep my end of the bargain and drive sober.

But a short way into the drive, Nicole, who had taken the first shift behind the wheel, looked over at me and whispered, "Joe, look at your hands." (She whispered so she wouldn't alarm Ally in the back seat.) I looked down and there in my lap, holding my cell phone, my hands were shaking uncontrollably. Needless to say, Nicole stayed behind the wheel the rest of the way.

My shaking continued throughout the whole trip: as we arrived in Tallahassee and found something to eat, as we moved Ally into her apartment, and as we had breakfast with Ally the next morning before saying goodbye. I was also sweaty, irritable, and short with everyone.

Before heading back, Nicole and I parked in front of a liquor store until it opened at noon. I went in, bought a few shots, brought them back to the car, and drank them—and immediately the shakes, sweats, and dizziness subsided.

I'll never forget how Nicole and I looked at each other, because the same crystal-clear thought came to each of us. Drinking was no longer a choice for me. *I had to drink.* I definitely, undeniably, had a problem. I was powerless over alcohol. I needed help.

It was a quiet drive back to Palm Beach.

During the following days and weeks, spiritually, I was lost. I was dying inside. I was filled with fear, shame, and guilt. For so many years, I had been selfish, flawed, and sinful. I had ignored God for decades. How could I possibly ask him to help me now? I shook my head, knowing I couldn't. I was completely lost.

Chapter 3: Nicole's Nightmare

I surrender every fear that I have to you. – the
SURRENDER PRAYER

As I mentioned in Chapter 1, I remember nothing from the night of my collapse on my living room floor through the nine weeks I spent in one institution after another. It was my family that lived the nightmare, especially my wife, Nicole. I've asked her to tell you about it:

"Please Come Help Me"

The night Joe collapsed, literally losing his mind for those nine horrible weeks, began ordinarily enough. We went out to one of our favorite restaurants, Café Chardonnay. We had decided to celebrate the New Year on December 30. That way we would avoid the New Year's Eve crowds and madness.

It's a charming place for a date night. Joe didn't eat much, however, filling up on drinks instead. We went home, watched some TV, and then I went upstairs to bed while he stayed in the living room to drink some more.

I had been asleep for about an hour when my cell phone rang. It was charging on the floor by our bed. I answered and Joe said, "Nicole, something is wrong. Please come help me." I hurried down to find him half-lying on the sofa, garbling his words, and hardly able to stand on his own feet. He had to lean on me to get to our car. I raced him to Jupiter Medical Center, they put him in a wheelchair and rolled him into the emergency room, and then I drove home because I could not enter due to the COVID protocols.

I was terribly frightened Joe was having a stroke, but all I could do was wait for my phone to ring.

A Frightful Deterioration

About an hour later, I got a call from the hospital with the good news that Joe was not having a stroke, but they didn't know what was wrong with him. It would be a long time before I got any more good news. Joe's condition deteriorated quickly. Within a couple of days, his body went into shock from alcohol withdrawal. He had the tremors and sweats, was in and out of consciousness, and declining fast. They put him in the ICU, and it was touch and go for a while, very scary.

Joe's mind continued to get worse as well. He didn't know us. His words made no sense. He began to hallucinate. They put some very powerful antipsychotic drugs into him, but to no apparent effect.

His demeanor grew combative, even aggressive, toward hospital staff and other patients, so much so that they put him in restraints for a while. He wouldn't eat. His muscles atrophied from extensive bedrest. He had no bathroom skills and could not dress himself.

I tried to FaceTime him with the help of the nurse by his bed, but I mostly ended up just talking to her as Joe lay there catatonic. It was heartbreaking.

I had to have so many difficult conversations in those days with family members, including Joe's aging father in Chicago, explaining the extent of Joe's drinking and the deterioration he was undergoing. They were all supportive. Joe's father and our children tried to call Joe (they couldn't go see him because of COVID), hoping their contact would help him in some way, but it was fruitless: That strange voice on the other end of the line, rambling confusedly, was disheartening.

I don't know what I would have done without Joe's Aunt Gerry during this time. She's a nurse and translated doctor-speak for me. More importantly, she was an emotional godsend. Her words to me were so beautiful, so supportive and comforting. I leaned on her so much. We ended up calling each other constantly, even early mornings before I left for work.

Institution after Institution….

The doctors at Jupiter decided they had better send Joe to a rehab center before he lost all his motor skills, so on January 21, after three weeks and no certain diagnosis, they transferred him to Manor Care, an assisted living facility. Again, because of COVID I could not visit him. But I heard vividly how he began stripping down and walking naked through the halls, moaning for a drink.

Two weeks later, he was sent to Beach House, an addiction treatment center. He was a misfit from the beginning, not able to participate coherently in group meetings. So it was on to Palm Beach Gardens Medical Center, another hospital. Here he had a new set of doctors and a new round of tests, but Joe's exact diagnosis continued to elude them. Their conclusion was that he had alcohol-related dementia.

At Palm Beach Gardens, however, I was able to go

see Joe in person! I was so incredibly grateful. I would go by and see him after work, just to sit with him or to take him something to eat. Just think how you would feel if your husband or wife suddenly encountered the worst crisis of their life, but you, at that very moment when they needed you most, were kept from seeing them! That is what happened to Joe and me. It meant so much to me to be able to go in and see him again.

At Palm Beach Gardens his hallucinations got really wild. Some of them were horrible, which I won't relate. But some were humorous. For example, he would imagine that we were on an exotic cruise and say, "This is such a beautiful view. Can you pass me the menu? I want to see what I'm going to order before the waitress comes back." Another time he said to me, "Oh, you brought your twin. You two are so adorable! Let me get a picture." Once he winked at me and said, "Word on the street is you're quite the stripper. Thanks for bringing in some extra income."

But the humor was fleeting. The next moment he would be staring off into space, fidgeting uncontrollably, scratching all over. He was like some crazy, frightening character from *One Flew Over the Cuckoo's Nest.*

The Weight of the World

Looking back, I really don't know how I survived those weeks. I felt the weight of the world was on my shoulders. In addition to my burden for Joe's welfare, my responsibility for his healthcare decisions, and my personal loneliness at his absence, I still had to live my day-to-day life: face 20 kindergartners for seven hours each day, relate professionally to coworkers, be a stepmother to Ally and Colin, take care of the house, buy groceries, pay bills. All of this while either in tears or on the verge of them every waking hour. I shudder remembering it all. I don't know how I did it.

Wernicke-Korsakoff Syndrome

After Palm Beach Gardens, Joe was sent for one more rehab attempt at another care center (Palm Garden of West Palm Beach), but they weren't any better equipped to handle a psychotic patient than the other places, and at this point Joe was "Baker-Acted" into St. Mary's Medical Center's psychiatric ward.

It was the doctors at St. Mary's who finally diagnosed his condition: Wernicke-Korsakoff Syndrome. Alcohol had so re-wired his brain that he was in a state of perpetual memory loss, not able to remember one day, or perhaps even one minute, after the other. Out of 100 patients who develop the disorder, 20 will die, 75 will have severe lifelong disabilities, and the remaining "lucky" 5 will have some manner of defect and will *never* fully recover.

"Mrs. McGivney," the doctors at St. Mary's told me, "you need to prepare yourself and your family. Your husband will likely be like this for the rest of his life." Then they had another bombshell for me: "But he can't stay here. This is a hospital, not a long-term care facility. You must find a permanent location for him."

I was devastated. Our whole family was devastated.

But I had no time to grieve or catch my breath. I had to find a place for Joe, and we were running out of institutions in South Florida. I would have to scour the whole state, even the nation, for a place to take him in—with no idea how to pay for it all. Then a caseworker who was helping me contacted the Retreat, another local substance abuse facility, and they graciously agreed to take Joe in. But they stipulated: "Only for 30 days. Just to give you time to find a permanent solution."

So on March 5, 2021, Joe was transferred from St. Mary's to the Retreat....

Awakening

... where, the next morning, he woke up completely well.

But I didn't know it yet. Joe himself (after waking up completely well) was walking around the Retreat in a daze that day, trying to figure out what was going on. It wasn't until later day that I talked to him, after he had been rushed to the JFK Medical Center because his blood pressure dropped too low. A male nurse from JFK called me. "Would you like to talk to your husband?" he asked.

"Well. Sure. I guess," I said, because I couldn't imagine what kind of conversation we would have. Just days ago, Joe was saying to me, "What do you mean you're my wife? I don't know anyone named Nicole."

"Hi, Honey," Joe said when he came on the line. "Don't worry, I'm fine. I was just dehydrated. They're putting some fluids in me, and I'll be back at the Retreat tonight."

I was astonished. Here he was having a completely normal conversation with me, like nothing had ever happened, like the old Joe. He was speaking clearly, making sense, and knew he was talking to his wife! He had even remembered my phone number and asked the nurse to call me.

"Can I come see you?" I asked.

He asked the nurse, then said, "Yes, you can come."

I quickly hung up, got on I-95, and drove to the hospital. I had to see this Mystery in person.

I entered the emergency room, and, sure enough, there Joe stood by his gurney, looking normal and cheerful, wearing blue jeans and a hospital gown. "Hi," he said, "I missed you so much! Thank you for coming. You look great. How are you?" He opened his arms for a hug.

I returned the hug, but very mechanically. I had built a protective shell around my heart these nine weeks, I had been hurt so much. Besides, I just couldn't believe what I was seeing.

"Joe, what's happening? Just the other day you didn't know who I was! You asked for documentation to prove I was your wife. You thought I was the Uber driver coming to take you to the airport. Now you're perfectly normal! What has happened?"

"What are talking about?" he said. "What do you mean? Something happened to me?"

I was shocked. He had no recollection of anything from those nine weeks.

I sat down in a chair by his gurney to collect my thoughts, then began to fill him in on everything that had happened—his collapse, the hospitals and institutions, the hallucinations.

He looked at me in bewilderment. "I have no memory of anything," he said. "I'm so sorry, Nicole. Ashamed. I didn't know I was so out of control. I'll try to make it up to you." He smiled at me. "I'm so happy to see you, though. I love you so much."

I could not return a smile with the same warmth. As thrilled as I was to see him well, I was so angry at him, so hurt, for all he'd done to us—to our marriage, to me, to himself, to our beautiful children. All because of alcohol! I was just so heartbroken, and I felt completely disrespected, pushed away, and not a priority at all.

Unloved and uncared for.

I would not be able to snap my fingers and forget it all.

Chapter 4: "I Can't Do This Anymore"

I surrender every person in my life to you. – the
SURRENDER PRAYER

I was able to talk Nicole into taking me back to the Retreat after they got my blood pressure stabilized. I learned later that she almost declined, nervous to be in the car with me alone. Yes, she had just spent two hours with "Normal Joe," but what if "Crazy Joe" appeared again on the drive over? But she gave me the ride. I asked her to stop at a convenience store on the way back, and I went in and bought a carton of Marlboro Lights. I had been on and off again when it came to my smoking, but I felt like I really needed a cigarette now.

My head was still spinning from everything Nicole had just told me about the last nine weeks—my collapse, my psychosis, my institutional odyssey. How could all that have happened? How could I do those things, be that way? I couldn't wrap my head around it, and guilt, shame, and fear weighed heavily on me.

When she pulled into the Retreat parking lot, I looked at her and said, "Nicole, you've always been there for me. It's my turn now."

I can't remember if she had much, or anything, to say in response.

The Retreat

I went inside and was welcomed back with an

obligatory full body strip search. They were making *completely* sure I wasn't smuggling any contraband—drugs or booze—back in with me. The staff member who took me into a private room to search me said, "You know the drill."

"What do you mean?" I said.

"Just like yesterday when they brought you in," he said.

But I had no memory of it at all.

The Retreat was an upscale place. It had a state-of-the-art fitness center and a full gym with an indoor basketball court and pickleball nets set up for play, as well as a library stocked with books and musical instruments, including a piano, guitars, and bongo drums. There was also a large cafeteria where, I would soon learn, top-notch meals were served—always fresh and under the watchful eye of an executive chef. The meals were something I came to look forward to. But my favorite part was that they had a cappuccino machine and an ice cream freezer that was stuffed with all-you-can-eat ice cream bars. I was burning through about four ice cream bars a day.

Other than the cafeteria, where all 75 to 80 patients ate together, the main gathering place was the smoking hut, an outdoor tiki hut-like building, with no walls, but a roof for shade, and a bunch of benches and seats that spilled out onto the grounds. Even people who did not smoke congregated at the smoking hut.

I must say that the camaraderie at the Retreat was comforting. One of the first things a new patient was asked, including me, was, "How did you end up here?" and for the most part people shared their stories openly. No one would say, "Wow, you're a horrible human being," because each one of us had our own terrible tale; we were all in the same leaky boat. Some of the patients were as young as 18, some were senior citizens. Some carried themselves professionally, some were just off the mean streets. A common bond of failure and pain and hope united us. It was very comforting at that time in my life.

My Only Mission

The first chance I got I sat down with my lead therapist, whom I'll call Teresa, and my first question to her was, "When am I getting out of here?" Because my only thought was, *I've got to get out of here as quick as I can and get back to Nicole and convince her to stay with me.* That was my only goal at the Retreat, my only mission. The reason I put one foot in front of the other.

Teresa checked her sheet. "Joe, you're here until April 5th," she said.

"No way," I said. "There's no chance I'm staying here until April 5th. That's almost a month from now."

"Joe, you're sick. You need to be here for a month."

"Well, I'm not staying for a month. You can't keep me here."

"No, we can't. There's no barbed wire fence, no locks on the doors. But you would be leaving, as we say, AMA."

"AMA?" I said. "What does that mean?"

"Against medical advice," she said. "Which means that everything your insurance company has paid for so far, and will pay for going forward, will have to come out of your pocket—if you leave AMA." She smiled. "And the Retreat *will* collect."

"Oh," I said. That took the wind out of my sails. I could only imagine how much all this was costing. "Well, looks like I'm staying until April 5th."

But I really didn't think I'd have to stay that long. I was convinced I would be able to persuade them to let me out early for good behavior. I would be a model patient. With my lifetime of getting my way and charming people and persuading people for a living, I was convinced I would be able to get them to cut me loose at least two weeks early.

Didn't happen.

Going through the Motions

There were several different treatment tracks at the Retreat, and their schedules were posted on a wall by the lobby. There were tracks for a substance abuse group, a mental health group, a combination substance abuse/mental health group, a PTSD group for soldiers, and a combination PTSD/substance abuse group.

It would turn out that I was assigned to the substance abuse/mental health group. "Okay," I said. "Whatever." I was just going through the motions anyway. Just biding my time until I could get out and get eyeball to eyeball with Nicole.

Later others in the group would say to me, "It sounds like you just have a drinking problem. Why aren't you over there with those guys?" I told them I didn't know, wondering again about all the crazy things I must have done during my "blank" nine weeks.

The days developed into a rhythm. We woke up early for breakfast at seven or seven-thirty, and then came the morning therapy sessions, group meetings covering topics such as accountability, how to deal with conflict in constructive ways, and how to heal our pain and soothe our anxieties without the use of drugs and alcohol. Occasionally, we would have a one-on-one session with our lead therapist.

After lunch, more sessions followed, or sometimes we had special activities, such as art room time. This was a room full of brushes and paints and easels, and you were free to do your thing, express yourself. They also had color by number materials if you didn't want to think too hard about it. I'm no artist by any means, but I painted a rock with the three words I'd seen on someone's t-shirt: "Faith, Hope, and Love." I didn't know at the time that those words came from a passage from the Gospels, but they made an impression on me. Outside there was a little rock garden, where I put my offering beside others.

It's interesting how this art room really connected with some of the patients. There was one man who'd never painted a stroke in his life, but when he sat down with a brush in his hand, these incredibly beautiful paintings came out of him.

We were also given free time in the afternoons, and I decided that every other day I would go to the gym and workout, do some lifting and some cardio, like I used to do. I was amazingly weak from all my time in bed, and I wanted to rebuild my strength. But my main motivation was to look the best I could to help convince Nicole to stay with me.

In the evenings, after dinner, patients would hang out by the smoking hut or in the TV room. There were no TVs in our bedrooms, or any other electronic distractions. I usually grabbed something from the library to read when it was time to head back to our rooms.

It was just before bedtime when something odd started happening to me. Some of the hallucinations that I had had during my nine lost weeks would suddenly flash in my mind. Some of the funny or odd ones, but also some of the horrifying ones. The troubling thing was, I couldn't tell, at least not right away, whether they were hallucinations or actual memories. For example, I had hallucinated that my dad had passed away and I had declined to go to his funeral just to save a few bucks. That caused me a lot of angst until I was able to confirm it wasn't true. There were several such hallucinations that masqueraded as memories in my mind in those days. It was always a relief to be able to debunk them with facts.

For the most part I was a model patient because I didn't want to do anything that would delay my release, but one time I lost it. Some evenings a local barber came into the Retreat to give haircuts for as little as $5, that is, basically as an act of charity, donating his time. I needed a haircut badly; I looked like a wild man. I signed up and got in line. As my turn approached, a staff member, a very young woman, pulled up the patient list and said, "I'm sorry, Mr. McGivney, but you can't get a haircut."

"What do you mean?" I said. "I signed up two days ago, and I've been waiting in line."

"Your therapist didn't approve your haircut," she said.

"What! I need a therapist to approve my haircut?" I lost it. "What kind of place is this?" I went off on that poor girl. This was just one more reason I needed to get out of there!

About 10 minutes later, I did go back and apologize profusely to the young woman, who was just doing her job. And afterwards I learned why I needed approval for a haircut. It was because just days before I had been locked up in the psych ward at St. Mary's, considered a danger to myself and others. They weren't quite ready to let me near a sharp pair of barber's scissors.

The Phone Call

No one was allowed to visit me at the Retreat because of COVID, but I was allowed a few calls to loved ones, but only for 10 or 15 minutes per call, and only in the presence of a therapist. About a week into my stay, I had a call scheduled with Nicole. It took place in the office of a therapist whom I will call Matt, a big, muscle-bound, military veteran with a U.S. flag and service medals on his wall. Matt, despite his appearance, had a disposition as kind and gentle as a puppy. He sat behind his desk and put us on speaker phone.

"Hi, Honey! It's sure great to talk to you." I said. "I miss you."

"Hello, Joe."

"How are you?" I asked.

"I'm fine."

"Good. Good," I said, but my heart sank, because already, even in this small talk, I could hear in her voice that this was not going to go well.

After a little more chit-chat, she cut to the chase. "Joe, you have no idea how happy I am you're doing so well. I can't even begin to say how happy I am for you." I could hear that she had started to cry. "But I can't do this anymore. You need to know that I've

32

already packed up. When you get home, the house will be empty. I will be gone, and I'm asking you to please just let me be. I can't do this anymore." She continued to cry.

I began to respond, to make my plea for her to stay, but Matt put up his hand and said, "Joe, stop." Then he said, "Nicole, let's hit the pause button here. You don't have to make any decisions today. Why don't we set up another call?"

"There won't be another call," Nicole said. "I can't do this anymore."

The call ended.

I sat there, tears streaming down my face. Because I knew Nicole. When she makes up her mind and takes a stand, nothing's going to change that. I could hear in her voice that she had made up her mind. "The house will be empty. I will be gone." I knew nothing I could say or do could change her mind.

My mission to get home and win Nicole back—to make up for all I had put her through—was over. The woman I loved was gone.

I put my head in my hands and sobbed. I was absolutely broken. My aching heart was a big black hole, and I was falling through it.

Chapter 5: Empty House

I surrender all sadness I am experiencing in my heart to you. – the SURRENDER PRAYER

As I sat there weeping in Matt's office, he said to me, "Joe, I'm so sorry." Then he said, "You know what? There's an AA meeting starting in five minutes, and you have to go."

I raised my head and cussed him. "Look at me!" I cried. "I'm a complete mess. Anyway, the AA meetings are optional. We don't have to go."

"Joe, they are optional, and you don't have to go. But, Joe"—he looked intently at me—"you have to go. Tonight."

"I can't! I'm—"

"Joe, just go."

And for some reason I did. I stood, exited his office, and walked down the long hall to the cafeteria. Inside, about 50 residents were seated around the big circular cafeteria tables. I had never been to an Alcoholics Anonymous meeting before, though the Retreat hosted three of them each week, Monday, Wednesday, and Friday nights. Volunteers from the community (recovering alcoholics themselves) ran them, one who chaired the meeting, one who told his or her story. I knew many other residents attended, but I always declined. "No thanks, I'm good," I would say, because my goal at the Retreat was not to get *sober* but to get *out*. To get back to Nicole and convince her to stay with me.

34

But that goal had come to nothing. Nicole would not be there when I got home.

I was completely broken, and the tears kept streaming down my face as I found a seat at one of the tables.

"I'm Terrified and I Need Help"

The meeting began with a reading of the Twelve Steps, which were printed on a large banner on the wall. Step One: "We admitted we were powerless over alcohol—that our lives had become unmanageable." *Well,* I thought as I heard the first step read, *here I am. I just lost my wife. I'm in a treatment facility. I don't remember the last two months. I'm pretty sure my life qualifies as unmanageable.*

Step Two: "We came to believe that a Power greater than ourselves could restore us to sanity." *Well,* I thought, *I came to this place from the psychiatric ward. 'Sanity' sounds like a good place to be.*

Step Three: "We made a decision to turn our will and our lives over to the care of God *as we understood Him.*" I didn't hear the rest of the steps as the import of this step settled on my heavy heart. *How do I do this? What would God want from me? Will he really take care of me? Why would God do anything for a sinner like me?*

I turned my attention to that night's speaker when he got up to tell his story. He was in his mid-40s, well-dressed, relaxed. He told how he had worked his way up in the casino business in Las Vegas, made a lot of money, and landed a prestigious job. But he said he had always felt something missing, an emptiness inside, and he tried to fill it up with alcohol to the point that it took control. I felt like he had climbed inside my brain and was reading my story. "I lost everything, my job, my money, my relationships," he said, "until I was living in my truck behind a convenience store, a loaded gun in my hand, ready to take my life." But that's when his family found him, intervened, and got him help.

He told of how he got sober, turned his life over to God, and started working the Twelve Steps. "Over time I got everything back, plus a peace I never knew before."

The volunteer chairing the meeting asked if anyone else had something to share, and though I had never been to an AA meeting before, I found myself on my feet, tearfully choking out the words, "My wife literally just left me and I'm terrified and I need help." Then I just shut up and cried. People brought me paper towels to wipe my face with, said kind things, hugged me.

I went to bed that night feeling like an 18-wheeler had rumbled over me, then backed up and parked itself on my gut. Everything inside me ached. I had lost my wife. I was an alcoholic. Thoughts of my past and present brought pain. Thoughts of my future, fear. I had raised my white flag at the AA meeting, admitting I had a problem and needed help. But now what?

All I knew, when I woke up the next morning, was that I had no choice but to try to figure out how to live without alcohol. The rest of my time at the Retreat I was a model patient, but for the right reason this time: to learn everything I could about staying sober. I made sure not to miss another AA meeting. My only glimmers of hope in those gloomy weeks came from the stories I heard the speakers share in those meetings and from the similar stories I read in the Big Book

(AA's basic text) in my room at night. Stories of people who had burned down their lives with alcohol like I had, but who, through the Twelve Steps and God, had found more beautiful, joyful, and peaceful lives than they ever imagined. I wanted that.

But hopeful stories were not my only motivation....

I was given a roommate after I had been at the Retreat for a few days, a smart and friendly young man, who went through the horrors of opiate and alcohol withdrawal right before my eyes. At times he would bundle up in a sweatshirt, jacket, and all his blankets and lay on his bed shivering and moaning in pain. "It feels like my skin is alive and jumping!" he said. An hour or so later I would come back in the room and find him sitting naked on a chair in the shower, running ice cold water over himself because he felt like his skin was on fire. All of this with one gut-wrenching vomit after another.

I knew that I had gone through my own detox at Jupiter Medical Center, one severe enough to land me in ICU, but I could not remember a bit of it. This young man's suffering, however, was burned indelibly on my mind, a graphic warning of what lay ahead of me if I did not stop drinking.

Discharge

The day before I was scheduled to be released from the Retreat, I had to meet with the discharge therapist, whose job it was to interview me and decide whether I got to go home or not. I had never met with this therapist before, but she had all of my paperwork at hand. She said, "Joe, what's your plan for when you get out? How are you going to stay on the right track?"

"Don't worry," I said, "I've got this."

Witness again the deceptive powers of alcoholism! After all I'd been through, all I'd learned, and all I still had to face, even now I apparently planned to just wing it when I got out.

She shook her head. "Joe, you don't 'got this'. You're sick. You need help."

She went on to explain that there were various programs that people released from a residential treatment center went into to ease their way back into the real world. For example, there were intense outpatient programs, in which you slept in your own home but came to the center in the day for therapy. Or there were sober-living houses where you did the opposite, slept in the sober house and went out to your job in the day. And there were other options.

"I'm not doing any of that," I told her flat out. "I've got this."

"Joe, I can't tell you how many people have sat in that chair and used those exact words, 'I've got this,' and are right back here a week later, a month later, a year later." She sighed. "I'm going to release you, but I want you to promise me—no, I want you to promise *yourself*—that you will do two things. First, get to an AA meeting immediately and get a sponsor who will walk you through the Twelve Steps. Second, I want you to get on your computer, go to Google and search "SURRENDER PRAYER" in all caps. There are several versions of the SURRENDER PRAYER, so find one that resonates with you. Print it off and pray it every single day. Will you promise yourself you will do those two things?"

I liked how she asked me to promise *myself* I would do those two things. I had not only broken so many promises to others through the years, but also to myself. I was so familiar with that morning-after guilt and shame. This time had to be different.

"I can do that," I said.

I also met with the staff nurse before I was discharged, and she told me, "I'm going to prescribe some anti-craving medicine for you."

It dawned on me that I hadn't been craving alcohol ever since that first AA meeting. "I don't need it," I said. "I'm not craving alcohol."

"Well, at least take the prescription in case you change your mind," she said.

I took it, but I never filled that prescription.

The nurse also gave me my Psychiatric Discharge Summary from St. Mary's, where later I could read all about the "acute psychosis" of one "McGivney, Joseph P" in all its particulars. It was eerie reading.

Pity Party

The next day they drove me home in the Retreat van. There was no one to come and pick me up. All I had with me were the clothes on my back and a duffel bag with a few things Nicole had packed for me. My emotions were mixed. I was relieved to be going home, to be leaving the regimented routine of a treatment center. But I was fearful about the future: going home to an empty house, trying to live without booze. It was easy being sober at the Retreat, where alcohol was not an option. But what about when I'm out on my own, and it is an option? When we pulled out of the Retreat parking lot, I noticed the liquor store that is literally across the street from the Retreat. When we neared my neighborhood, I noticed the liquor store where I had bought all those mini-bottles of vodka. They were both open.

The van dropped me off in front of my house at about 1:00 in the afternoon.

I went inside the empty house.

I dropped my duffel bag and wandered around downstairs a bit. Then I went upstairs, went in our bedroom, and opened the clothes closet. All of Nicole's clothes were gone. There was no sign she had ever been there. That was a desolate moment, a lump the size of my heart in my throat.

I went into my upstairs office and plopped down in front of my laptop. A sizable to-do list had accumulated over three absent months. I answered emails, paid bills, balanced accounts. I also had to contact my employer, who was still shut down for COVID and thus had not, thankfully, felt my absence enough to fire me. And I had to contact my lawyer about the divorce proceedings, which Nicole had already set in motion.

Alone in the house—not only was Nicole gone, but Ally was away at college and Colin was staying with his mother—I started feeling sorry for myself, even a little angry. Three months gone and no one home to meet me! I thought of my Aunt Gerry (the one who was a nurse and who had often called Nicole during my sickness to encourage her). I had always been her pet nephew and knew I could always count on her to be on my side. I decided to call her up and have a little pity party with her.

I was so happy when she picked up. It was nice to talk to someone who loved me. After a few preliminaries, I said, "Can you believe Nicole is leaving me? How could she do it?"

Then Aunt Gerry, this beautiful little Irish lady, said to me, "Joe, nothing could be further from the truth!"

That wasn't what I wanted to hear.

She wasn't finished: "Do you have any idea of the pain you've put that woman through over the last few months? The pain you've put me through, your father through, your children! Who do you think you are?" She went on to describe for me all the gory details of the nightmare I'd put my family through. Nicole, that day in the JFK emergency room, had only given me the big picture. Aunt Gerry showed me all the ugly closeups. "Of course, she left you!" she concluded.

"I really had no idea," I said, overwhelmed with shame and guilt. It was plain that Nicole had loved me faithfully through every dark minute, and it was plain that it was completely my fault that she had finally left.

Aunt Gerry and I had a long, long conversation, during which she explained Wernicke-Korsakoff Syndrome to me, because this was the first time I'd heard the term. She said, "Joe, *no one* gets over Wernicke-Korsakoff Syndrome like you have."

"What do you mean?"

"No one who has progressed to full-blown Korsakoff Psychosis, like you did, suddenly wakes up well one day."

"I don't understand. What are you saying, Aunt Gerry?"

After a pause: "I'm saying there's no medical explanation for what happened to you."

That was the first time I seriously considered the question: *How did I get well? How was I crazy for nine weeks and suddenly woke up one day normal as ever?* As I said goodbye to her, I knew I was going to have to ponder that question.

But for now, a more pressing question required attention: *How am I going to stay sober?*

I thought of my two promises....

Chapter 6: Promises Kept

I surrender all anxiety and worry I have to you. –
the SURRENDER PRAYER

My first promise to keep: get to an AA meeting immediately and get a sponsor.

Promise Number One

The person who came to my mind was Chris B., a realtor who had helped me buy a home. We were just acquaintances, but at one point had gone out to lunch together. I had ordered a drink and asked if I could get him one, and he said, "No, I'm good. I'm in recovery." He was the only person I knew who had openly acknowledged being in recovery, so I called him up and said, "Hey, I remember you saying that you're in recovery. Are you in AA?"

"Yeah," he said.

"I really need some help. I want to go to an AA meeting."

"Cool," he said. "There's one at Club Oasis tomorrow night at 5:30. Meet me in the parking lot."

The funny thing was, I had driven by Club Oasis literally hundreds of times over the years. It's right outside my neighborhood, tucked off the road in a little wooded area. But I had never imagined it was an Alcoholics Anonymous clubhouse (an AA clubhouse is a building dedicated entirely to AA meetings). In fact, passing its sign on the road, I had occasionally thought, *Club Oasis? I wonder what goes on there? Probably a swingers' club.* Who knew what might pop into my head in those days.

I met Chris in the parking lot. He's a good-looking guy, a couple years older than me and very fit—a swimmer, cyclist, and near-par golfer. "Glad you called," he said, and led me inside, past groups of people who were hanging around outside the entrance and chatting. He took me up to a counter which functioned as a sort of a concession stand and ordered me a cup of coffee, then we went inside the main meeting room.

Chris sat us right up front, opposite the table where the chairman and the speaker sat with a microphone between them. As others filed in, Chris took the opportunity to make a couple of points to me. "Joe, did you notice anything about the parking lot?"

"What do you mean?" I said.

"There were vehicles of every type, from Escalades to junkers and even a couple bicycles. Sometimes one man rolls up in a Bentley, believe it or not. And do you notice anything about the people in here?"

I looked around the room. There were people of every age, every race, men and women. A couple of guys in suits might have come straight from their bank jobs. Others were in t-shirts and blue jeans. Others had hair looking like they'd just rolled out of bed. Some looked happy, with a kind of glow around them. Some looked like the world had taken a stick to them that day.

"All kinds," Chris said. "Just people who want to recover from alcoholism."

I realized this was my first AA meeting in the "real world." At the Retreat, all the attendees had been my fellow residents, with little else to do with their nights. But all these people, from all walks of life, had a million and one other things they could be doing. But they had chosen to come to a meeting.

I don't remember much about that first meeting. I was on sensory overload, overwhelmed. At one point the chairman asked, as is customary in AA meetings, "If there's anyone here who is still 'counting days,' please raise your hand, so we can get to know you." "Counting days" means you're still in your first 90 days of sobriety, in which it's highly recommended that you attend "90 meetings in 90 days." Chris had to nudge me to raise my hand. When I did, I noticed a number of other newbies in the room. Other people in their first scary days; other people wondering if they could pull this off.

Afterward, Chris took me to the counter in the lobby and got me a list of meetings. "Which one are you going to tomorrow?" he said rather pointedly.

I looked at the list and saw that there was no excuse for not making time for a meeting. There were something like six each day, seven days a week.

"I tell you what," Chris said. "I'm going to come to the 5:30 meeting again tomorrow night. Come with me to the 5:30 meeting."

"Okay. I will. I'll do that."

It was either at that meeting the next night, or the one the following night, that I heard the chairman say, "If anyone's willing to be a sponsor, please raise your hand." This request is another regular part of an AA meeting. Chris, again sitting beside me, raised his hand.

"Will you be my sponsor?" I asked him.

He cracked a smile. "I thought you'd never ask."

After the meeting, he took me into the lobby and bought me my own copy of the Big Book. "We've got some work to do," he said, and assigned me some pages to read. "Meet me here tomorrow at 5:00, thirty minutes before the meeting, and we'll start walking through the Twelve Steps."

And that began my journey through the Twelve Steps. Over the following months, Chris and I often sat at one of the picnic tables on Club Oasis' outer deck, under a thatched roof, and worked through the steps. And I mean it was *work*. But my transformation—I realize now, looking back—was underway. Gradually my hope began to grow, and my healing began to come. Sobriety was becoming a part of who I was.

Promise Number Two

My second promise to keep was to pray the SURRENDER PRAYER every day of my life.

Those first few mornings were awkward and, frankly, a little scary. Who was I to talk to God? But I began with a "gratitude list," something I had learned at the Retreat. We were taught that no matter how horrible our life might be at the moment, there was always something to be thankful for, and we should think about those things. So that's how I began my prayer ritual each morning, listing the reasons I had to be thankful:

"Dear God, I thank you that I'm alive.

"I thank you that I'm sober today.

"I'm thankful for my healing.

"I thank you for my wonderful children."

The amazing thing was how my "gratitude list" would just naturally expand into my "conversation with God" time, as I called it, where I found myself talking to him just as I would a best friend, which, of course, is who he wants to be to each of us. I know that theologically now, but at the time I discovered it accidentally, just by experiencing it through my "conversation" with him.

Sometimes it was really beautiful, and my conversation with him would carry me out to the beach, watching him paint a new sunrise, my feet in the sand, the breeze on my face. My problems seemed smaller at times like that, and those moments, too, were part of the healing process.

Sometimes I would pull up the SURRENDER PRAYER on my phone right there on the beach, and read it word for word out loud:

God, my Father, I thank you for all that you are, and all that you do for me through your son Jesus Christ. I praise you for my life, for your mercy and for your Eucharist. In Jesus' name, Father, I place myself entirely in your Heart. I surrender to you my whole self, my heart, my mind, my memory, my imagination, my will, my emotions, my passions, my body, my sexuality, my desire for human approval, my weaknesses, my desires, my sins.

I surrender every person in my life to you. I surrender every situation in my life to you. I surrender every relationship I am in to you. I surrender every concern I have to you. I surrender every fear I have to you. I surrender every doubt I have to you. I surrender all confusion I have to you. I surrender all sadness I am experiencing in my heart to you. I surrender all my wounds to you. I surrender all anxiety and worry I have to you. I surrender all that deceives me in my heart to you. I trust you to care for me and others in a perfectly loving way.

As I have emptied myself, and surrendered everything to you, I ask you now, Father, to fill me with your Holy Spirit and all the gifts and fruits of your Spirit. Holy Spirit, you are the source of love, hope, joy, peace, patience, goodness, gentleness, tenderness, faithfulness, humility, and self-control. Purify my desires. Help me to open my heart to you. Help me to become perfectly receptive as a pure child. Help me to believe in your love for me. Help me to hope in your love. Help me to receive from the Most Sacred Heart of Jesus all grace and virtues necessary for me to become the person you created me to be. I ask this in the Name of Jesus Christ, Your Son, God Almighty Father.

O Most Holy Immaculate Virgin Mary. I entrust this prayer to your Heart, and ask you to press it to your wounded heart and intercede for me to your Son Jesus. Please help me to be as you are, a perfect disciple, an obedient servant, a true child of God. Amen.

Day by day, I felt a little closer to God. Day by day, my healing deepened.

Battles

But not without struggle—for four decades alcohol had been my daily companion, and it wasn't going to let go of me without a fight.

I remember, not long after starting to work through the steps with Chris, that he invited me to a Master's viewing party at his big, beautiful house. I showed up and found a bunch of people from AA there to watch the golf tournament, one of the most prestigious in the sport. They were just hanging out, smiling and laughing, and having real conversations with each other. "How are *you* doing, Joe? What's going on in your life?" Grown-up talk like that. All without a glass of booze in sight.

And I was horribly uncomfortable! I literally did not know how to behave without alcohol. What to say, what to do. It was just totally foreign to me to socialize without a drink in my hand. After about an hour, I went up to Chris and said, "I've got to go, man. Gotta go take care of something." I just had to get out of there. I left and drove back to my empty house and distracted myself somehow or other—but I didn't drink.

Another time, I was driving home from a meeting when out of nowhere an overwhelming feeling of dread came over me. My heart started pounding, my breath racing. I felt like the world was going to crash and burn around me. As soon as I got home, I called Chris and told him about it.

"Joe," he said, "it happens. It's not new to you. It's a part of the healing process. It will probably happen again."

"What do I do?"

"Either go back to another meeting or drop to your knees and pray."

After I hung up, I dropped to my knees and prayed the SURRENDER PRAYER. The nameless dread slowly drifted away. That was the moment I realized it's okay to pray more than one time a day!

One night I was sitting watching TV when another toxic emotion hit me square in the face. I suddenly remembered a man who had tried to harm someone near and dear to me. Somehow I hadn't even thought of him during my "moral inventory" work in Step Four. But now he was front and center in my mind, and my muscles tensed, my blood boiled, and I literally almost jumped up off the couch to hunt him down, just like I had plotted to do before my collapse. I was totally enraged.

But I had learned as a part of Step Four that if we ourselves want to be forgiven, we must be willing to forgive those who have wronged us. As the Big Book says, "Resentment...destroys more alcoholics than anything else." I immediately began to pray the Lord's Prayer (which we pray at the end of every AA meeting), especially the line, "Forgive us our trespasses, as we forgive those who have trespassed against us." And eventually I said, "Lord, I forgive this man. I let it go. You're the Judge, not me." And, again, those toxic emotions gradually faded away. By forgiving him, I was really the one being freed. It's a part of the healing process.

Back to Church?

Step Three, "turning our will and lives over to God" (which I'd almost stumbled over at that first AA meeting at the Retreat), was becoming the heartbeat of my life. I was learning that being close to God was not only the key to sobriety, but also the secret to joy and peace. And I wanted more of him, which led to the thought: *Shouldn't I go back to church?*

Frankly, I was afraid to attend Mass after all these years. So I started by visiting a big nondenominational church in our area called Christ Fellowship. My daughter had joined the youth group at Christ Fellowship while in high school, and had really liked it. Though she had been baptized as a Catholic, I was just happy she was finding some faith somewhere, because at that time she certainly wasn't getting it from me. So that's the church I slipped into one Sunday morning, a megachurch where a lone visitor didn't stick out like a sore thumb. It was a marvelously positive experience. There was an encouraging message, everything was about Jesus, and I left feeling fabulous.

But something inside me kept nudging me toward my Catholic roots, so one Sunday I worked up the courage and drove to St. Peter's Catholic Church in Jupiter, about ten minutes from my home. It wasn't the cold, dark, "fire-and-brimstone" church of my boyhood memories, but a place that was all about God's love, with beautiful music and choirs, and—about the third or fourth Sunday I attended—a message directly from God for me.

That message came to me in Father Don's homily about "what makes a good Catholic." He ended his homily by saying, "Heaven is not for the perfect. Heaven is for the forgiven." It was as though Heaven opened for me at that moment, and the spiritual peace I had always been looking for—that everyone is looking for—descended on me like the snow-white dove of Scripture. I realized my Heavenly Father had accepted me because of his goodness, not mine.

I was home.

Chapter 7: You're a Miracle!

I surrender all that deceives me in my heart to you. – the SURRENDER PRAYER

I heard someone say, "Never once have I dedicated an hour of my time to an AA meeting and walked out and said, 'That was a waste of time.' In every meeting I've heard something that in some way has helped me stay sober or become closer to God." I was finding that to be true in my own life. I had come to love those Club Oasis meetings, and I always walked away with some new gem in my mind or in my heart.

Just One Drink?

It wasn't only the inspiring stories that I heard in the meetings that motivated me, stories of people who had reclaimed their lives through God and the Twelve Steps. Those stories of hope were wonderful, and I never tired of hearing them. But "relapse stories" also played a role, stories of people who had gotten sober, sometimes for decades, but at some point decided, *You know what? I can have a drink. Just one*—and proceeded to burn their lives down all over again with alcohol, reaching a place deeper and darker than they had been in before.

One such story was told by a retired police officer. He had married early in life, had children, worked his career, until alcohol gradually took control. His wife left him, his kids wouldn't speak to him, his career suffered—the whole package. Hitting bottom, he turned to God and AA and got sober. He stayed sober 20 years, in the process rebuilding his relationship with his kids, meeting another woman and falling in love, and getting married.

He had a Thursday night date ritual with his new wife. They would go to their favorite restaurant, order their favorite dishes. He would order water or some soft drink (because he was now sober), and his wife, of European background, would order one Heineken, which she usually wouldn't even finish. That was their Thursday night ritual for years.

Then one Thursday night, sitting at their table, he thought, *That beer looks great. I'm going to have one tonight. Just one.* And he called the waiter over and ordered the beer.

He did stop at one that first night, but over the next seven days, until their next Thursday night dinner, he could think of nothing but that beer. He was so obsessed with it that he could hardly work. When Thursday came and his wife ordered her beer, he ordered one too. After drinking it down in a few minutes, he waved the waiter over and ordered another. Then another…. In a matter of months, his alcoholism had taken complete control again, and one more time he burned down his life.

Stories like that were bright red flags to me. I knew, being the kind of drinker I am, that just one drink and I would be off to the races. *I would not stop.* One shot of vodka and I'd be setting my life on fire again.

"What about Me?"

In addition to attending meetings and working through the steps, I was looking to make a career change. My employer at the time was still shut down for COVID, and my income had dropped dramatically, so I decided to pursue a new role with another investment firm, one that specialized in helping families and small business owners. The competition, however, was stiff, and their hiring process the most grueling of my career. I interviewed with recruiters, fellow financial advisors, a compliance lawyer, regional managers, administrators—something like eight different inquisitions over a number of weeks. It was a tough, thorough, and *long* process.

I'll never forget the day that I finally received a call from the recruiter: "Check your email, Joe. I just sent you an offer letter! Read it and get back to me as soon as possible. We want to get you onboard as quickly as we can. Congratulations!"

"Woo-hoo!" I shouted as I hung up the phone, and started dancing all over my home office high-fiving myself. I was literally jumping up and down and shouting, "I've got this!" *Wow, I beat out all those other candidates. I must be really impressive.* If my arms had been long enough, I would have knocked myself flat on my face from all the pats on my own back. "Woo-hoo!"

Then I heard a gentle whisper, not out loud but somehow to my soul: *"What about Me?"*

I immediately stopped jumping around and shouting. *"What about Me?"*

I knew it was the presence of God talking to me, and I quickly realized what I was doing: taking full credit for a blessing he had *given* me, a blessing I had been praying for. And it had not occurred to me to thank him at all!

I grabbed my copy of the SURRENDER PRAYER, fell to my knees, and started praying it. "Thank you, Father, thank you." And as I thanked him for the blessing, not taking full credit for it myself, my joy over it actually increased—my Heavenly Father was taking care of me! "Thank you, Father."

I'm amazed at how easily pride can lead me astray.

"You're a Miracle!"

One day, about a month after I'd started attending the AA meetings at Club Oasis, I showed up for an afternoon meeting rather than my usual 5:30 slot. It was another beautiful Florida afternoon and only about 20 people were present, and the woman chairing the meeting had an empty seat beside her at the table up front. I walked up and asked her, "Isn't there a speaker today?"

"My speaker cancelled," she said. Then: "You want to be the speaker?"

"What? Me?"

"How long have you been sober?" she asked.

I did some quick mental calculations: I'd collapsed December 30, been out of my head for nine weeks, spent a month at the Retreat, now another month had passed. "Four or five months," I said.

"That's good enough," she said. "You're the speaker."

I was completely unprepared, but I knew that every AA speaker addresses the same three questions in every meeting: First, how it was? That is, what was your life like before sobriety, what was your relationship with alcohol, and how did your disease progress? Second, what happened? That is, what led you to finally reach your bottom, raise your white flag, and accept that you were an alcoholic and needed help, how did you find your way to AA, and how did you work the steps? Third, how is it today? That is, when did your recovery click, what was your spiritual awakening, and what is your life like now? When it came time for me to speak, I simply answered those questions.

It was the first time I had shared my story in public, and the response was encouraging: rapt attention while I spoke and many kind words after. One of the people who came up to me after the meeting was a smartly dressed woman who identified herself as a psychiatrist. She said, "Do you know that you're a miracle?"

"Well, thank you," I said.

She shook her head. "No, you don't understand. I've treated Wet Brain patients throughout my career, and they don't recover like you have, and certainly not completely and overnight. You're a legitimate miracle, Joe, and as a doctor I don't throw around that term lightly."

"Wow," I said.

Here was another doctor saying there was no medical explanation for what happened to me. As you'll recall, I described in the first chapter how my primary care physician, Dr. Miller, said there was no scientific explanation for my recovery—for how a WKS patient could walk jauntily into her office, for how my liver enzyme reading could go from 209 (the highest she had ever seen) to 18 (right in the middle of the normal zone). I had also been to see a neurologist, who put me through a battery of mental exercises and declared, "By the grace of God, you're perfectly fine. I don't need to see you again." In addition, a cardiologist had given me a clean bill of health.

And now this psychiatrist, another sane and highly qualified professional, was telling me the same thing: There was no natural explanation for my healing.

Then what happened to me? I wondered, for the thousandth time since my awakening. *Why was I spontaneously and completely healed? How had it happened? Why had God chosen to heal me?*

The answer to that question finally came in one of my Saturday morning conversations with my Aunt Gerry. We've always been close. She is only about 10 years older than me, and she was a part of my life growing up. But these weekly calls began only after my release from the Retreat. I'm not sure she would admit it, but I think at first the calls were a means for Aunt Gerry, an RN, to check up on me: How did my week go? Was I seeing the doctors I needed to see? Was I still going to AA meetings? Since then, these calls have become a weekly tradition, a highlight of my week. We talk about life and faith and just generally solve all the world's problems. A short conversation for us is perhaps an hour.

That Saturday morning I had some good news for her: "Guess what, Aunt Gerry? I joined the Knights of Columbus."

The Knights of Columbus is a Catholic service organization for men. Locally, we do things like volunteer at the Special Olympics, take care of the yard at a home for unwed mothers, distribute Bibles in the prisons. Internationally, our organization comes to the aid of refugees (for example, providing shelter for

Ukrainians uprooted by the Russian invasion), assists with natural disaster relief, and helps with orphanages and missions. The Knights have about two million members worldwide in about 16,000 local "councils."

The reason I joined is because the Twelve Steps teach that part of our recovery process is to reach out and serve others. Plus, I have a personal connection to the Knights of Columbus. I happen to be related (as far as can be judged from surviving birth and baptismal records) to its founder, Father Michael McGivney. He began the organization at St. Mary's Church in New Haven, Connecticut, in 1882 to aid Catholic immigrants. He is even a candidate for sainthood in the Catholic church.

Despite my relation to him, I had never joined the Knights, and the only reason I did that week was a "coincidence." I needed a power washer for the exterior of my house, so I Googled up a local company and called the owner, who, when he heard my name, said, "McGivney? You don't happen to be related to Father McGivney of the Knights of Columbus, do you?"

"As a matter of fact, I am," I told him.

"Are you a Knight?"

"No."

"Why *not?*"

I didn't have a good answer for him. That week I did a little research, found a local council of the Knights at St. Peter's Catholic Church, where I was attending Mass at the time, and filled out the application for membership, which I had turned in the night before to the local council.

"I'm a Knight now, Aunt Gerry. A member of the Knights of Columbus."

I thought I'd hear her rejoicing over the phone, but, after a silent pause, I heard sobbing!

"Aunt Gerry, what's going on?"

"Joey," she said through her tears, "I've never told you this, but when you were sick, I was praying for you with all my heart. I was praying to God, to Jesus, to Mary and Joseph, to our deceased relatives—to anybody who would listen—and especially to Father McGivney of the Knights, our relative. I'm looking at his picture right now. I was praying for him to intercede for you to God. And he did, Joey, and you're healed!"

Wow! I was totally blown away. Was this the answer to my question? I had been healed because of prayer? Was it as simple, and profound, as that?

My secularly trained mind wanted to rebel at the idea, but facts were facts. I had been felled by Wernicke-Korsakoff Syndrome, in fact by its most extreme form, full-blown Korsakoff Psychosis. I had heard from multiple doctors that no one recovers from it like I had, and my own research had confirmed it. But one morning I was suddenly, completely well. What happened in-between? My Aunt Gerry's prayers.

Fireworks were going off inside my head. It was at once humbling, because I had nothing to do with my healing. I would still be trapped in a Korsakoff Psychosis nightmare if not for Aunt Gerry's prayers. But it was also so beautiful, because the love of God had intervened in my life and done something for me that only he could do. He himself had reached down and touched me and drawn me back from destruction.

As Pope Francis has said, "Our strength is prayer." Saint Pio (Padre Pio) put it this way, "Prayer is the best weapon we possess." And St. Thérèse of Lisieux declared: "Great is the power of prayer." I am living proof they are right.

But wait a minute! There was something else Aunt Gerry had said, something that gave me chills.

"Did you say you were praying to Father McGivney too?" I asked.

"Yes!" she said. "Our relative. The one who is a candidate for sainthood."

More fireworks went off in my head! Because it dawned on me that God may have had another reason for my healing, one that could play a role in the actual canonization of Father McGivney. In my research of the Knights of Columbus, I had been learning a lot about this remarkable man....

Chapter 8: Father McGivney

I trust you to care for me and others in a perfectly loving way. – the SURRENDER PRAYER

Father McGivney was, above all, a parish priest (in fact, *Parish Priest* is the title of his biography by historians Douglas Brinkley and Julie Fenster). He lived among and ministered to the poor Irish Catholics of Connecticut in the late 1800s, many of them, like his own parents, first-generation Potato Famine immigrants from across the sea. His father found work as a molder in a brass factory in Waterbury, Connecticut, and Michael himself, the eldest of 13 children, went to work in a spoon-making factory after his 13th birthday.

He expressed a desire for the priesthood, and at age 16 he entered Saint-Hyacinthe Seminary in Quebec. But when the tragic news of his father's early death reached him, he was forced to return home to support his mother and siblings. It took the intervention of the bishop of Hartford to restore Michael to his studies for the priesthood, and on December 22, 1877, he was ordained to the holy priesthood. In 1878, he was named curate of St. Mary's Church in New Haven, Connecticut.

He ministered during a time of Catholic persecution in America, and particularly in the Protestant bastion of New Haven. It was the day of "Irish need not apply" notices on shop doors. When a Catholic breadwinner died, often leaving 7, 8, 9 children behind, his widow

61

could be called into court to provide proof that she could financially support her children. If she could not, the state of Connecticut took the children away and put them in orphanages or up for adoption.

This was a great burden to young Father McGivney. Not only were dear families being broken up, but many children were being snatched away from their Catholic faith. In the fall of 1881, Father McGivney gathered two dozen men in the basement of St. Mary's Church and said, "We have to stop this." From these humble beginnings of literally "passing the hat" to keep Widow Kelly's or Widow Murphy's or Widow O'Conner's family together, grew the great Knights of Columbus fraternal order that today puts Christian love into action all over the world.

I was also interested to learn, from my research, that Father McGivney began a temperance league as well, St. Joseph's Total Abstinence and Literary Society, founded to combat the ravages of alcoholism that he saw in the community around him. This was a half-century before the formation of Alcoholics Anonymous.

Father McGivney's life on earth was cut short. In 1890, he came down with the Asian Flu that was devasting the lives of the people among whom he worked so closely (he was serving at St. Thomas Church in Thomaston, Connecticut, at the time). Complications led to a severe case of pneumonia, and Father McGivney died on August 14, 1890, two days after his 38th birthday.

But his influence was just beginning. It continues daily through the countless acts of service of two million Knights of Columbus members worldwide, as the Knights like to say, "Where there's a need, there's a Knight." In addition, and most exciting to me, Father McGivney is on the path to sainthood in the Catholic Church!

Steps to Sainthood

In the Catholic Church, there's a four-step path to sainthood. Step one is to be officially declared a Servant of God, which follows a rigorous examination of the candidate's life and doctrine. It is usually conducted by the Bishop of immediate jurisdiction, at the petition of the Catholic faithful. Father McGivney's Cause for Canonization was opened by Archbishop Daniel A. Cronin of Hartford on December 18, 1997, and Father McGivney was given the title Servant of God.

Step two is to be declared Venerable, or "Heroic in Virtue." The Pope must make this declaration, after he has reviewed sufficient evidence of the candidate's exemplary faith and service. Pope Benedict XVI declared Father McGivney a Venerable Servant of God on March 15, 2008.

Step three is to be declared Blessed, or Beatified. Advancing to this rare stage requires proof of at least one miracle having occurred as a result of the candidate's intercession in Heaven. This was provided for Father McGivney through a fetal hydrops case in Tennessee in 2015. A routine ultrasound revealed the malady, and medical professionals proceeded to give the child "zero percent" chance of survival. However, the father of the baby, Daniel Schachle, is a Knight of Columbus and well-acquainted with Father McGivney's legacy, and he and his wife prayed specifically for Father McGivney to intercede for their baby in Heaven. A follow-up ultrasound revealed no trace of fetal hydrops, and the baby boy is a joyful member of their family to this day. As a result of this miracle, Father McGivney was declared Blessed and was beatified on October 31, 2020.

This is the step at which Father McGivney's path to sainthood now rests. To attain to full sainthood, or canonization, there must be proof of *two* miracles having occurred through the candidate's intercession in Heaven. Which is what gave me the "chills" when Aunt Gerry told me on the phone that she had prayed to Father McGivney for my healing. Could *my miracle* possibly turn out to be the one that advances Father McGivney to sainthood? If so, this was bigger than me.

After Aunt Gerry and I hung up that Saturday morning, she went to fathermcgivney.org and noticed that there was a place on the website for people to report "favors"—that is, answers to prayer—that they believe have occurred through Father McGivney's intercession. She called me back and said, "Can I report your miracle to them?"

"Of course," I said.

Here's the message she sent them:

For nearly four months, my nephew experienced persistent delusional and psychotic behavior due to Wernicke-Korsakoff syndrome triggered by alcohol abuse. He was deemed permanently disabled, and the family was told he would spend the rest of his life needing 24/7 care. But after constant prayers to God and Father Michael McGivney, he literally awakened, to the shock of all his doctors and family. Four months later, he has returned to God, is alcohol free with the help of AA, and is an active Knight.

Notice, she did not give my last name or hers, but sent the message just as you read above. That same day she received this reply:

Thank you for sharing the good news about your nephew's recovery, and for your devotion to Blessed Michael McGivney. Would you be able to provide more details on this very unusual case? What is the name, age of your nephew and where does he live? Would he be willing to talk with me about his recovery? Are there others who were involved in his recovery?

The reply was from Brian Caulfield, who is the "Vice Postulator for the Cause of Blessed Michael McGivney," meaning he's the official in charge of weeding through the "favors" submitted on the site to find a second verifiable miracle to present to the Vatican on behalf of Father McGivney's canonization.

When Aunt Gerry shared his email with me, you might have thought I would be thrilled, but instead I freaked out! My thought was, *Oh no. They're going to want to know all about my story as a severe alcoholic. What about my reputation?* I was wondering how my new job with a respected investment firm might be affected.

A *Spiritual* Dilemma?

The next morning I went to Mass at St. Peter's, and afterward I hung around until Father Don had finished chatting with other parishioners, then I approached him.

"Father, I have a spiritual dilemma. Would it be possible to schedule a talk with you sometime? I need some help."

"What about right now?" he said and led me back into his office. We sat down and he said, "What's your spiritual dilemma?"

I pulled out my phone and showed him the email from the Vice Postulator. "I don't know what to do here," I said. "They're asking me to cooperate and tell my story. It could cause some real embarrassment for me. I know I should cooperate. After all, it's a pretty big deal, and it would be an honor to be a part of it. But what about me?"

Father Don looked straight at me and said, "So what exactly is your *spiritual* dilemma?"

What he said hit me like lightning. My mouth probably dropped open. I understood right away what he was saying. There was no *spiritual* dilemma, just a self-centered one. I had slipped back into selfish mode: *What's in this for me? Why should I cooperate?* Here God had performed a wonderful miracle in my life, one that could possibly play a role in Father McGivney's canonization, one that he intended to use to help others. And I was going to keep it to myself.

I stood up. "I get it, Father. There is no spiritual dilemma. I know exactly what I am supposed to do."

Not many days later, Brian Caulfield, the Vice Postulator, called me for a phone interview, and I was happy to give it. He asked for the details of my miracle, the same ones I've shared with you in this book, and then asked if he could talk to Dr. Miller, my primary care physician, and see my medical records. I had no problem with either request, so I made an appointment with Dr. Miller to ask her about it.

"How are you feeling, Joe?" she asked when I met her in her office.

"Great."

"That's wonderful. What can I do for you?"

I explained to her about the Vice Postulator reaching out to me, and how he wanted to speak to her, and asked, "Are you okay with that?"

"Certainly."

Then I asked her flat out: "Do you believe what happened to me was an actual miracle?"

She looked me straight in the eye and said, "Absolutely. There's no other way to explain it." Then she gave me her personal email address and cell phone number and said, "Feel free to pass these along. I'm happy to talk to them whenever they would like."

I thanked her, again so amazed that this cleared-eyed medical professional had not the slightest doubt about the miraculous nature of my healing. And of course I told Brian Caulfield that he was free to contact Dr. Miller.

And there, as far as my story's role in Father McGivney's canonization, is where I must leave it for now. That is all I know. The church is exceptionally thorough and circumspect when it comes to the entire sainthood process, with good reason. I also know that others have attested to "favors" through Father McGivney's intercession. I'm definitely not the only Father McGivney miracle. I am content to leave their stories and mine in God's hands. As I pray every day in my SURRENDER PRAYER, *I trust you to care for me and others in a perfectly loving way.*

Chapter 9: Infinite Power and Love

As I have emptied myself, and surrendered everything to you, I ask you now, Father, to fill me with your Holy Spirit and all the gifts and fruits of your Spirit. – the SURRENDER PRAYER

L ike so many others whose stories I've heard in one AA meeting after another, my life has not only been saved through the power of God and the Twelve Steps, it has become more beautiful and wonderful than it ever was before, more joyful and fulfilling than I ever imagined possible...

In the Presence

I was driving home from another A.A. meeting at Club Oasis when out of nowhere an overwhelming feeling of ecstasy and euphoria came over me. It enveloped me, body and mind, with peace, joy, and love. *What's going on here?* I thought. I even glanced at people in other cars, wondering, *Can they see this?*

Nothing unusual had happened at the Club Oasis meeting, or throughout that day. I began that morning with my usual prayer ritual of gratitude and surrender, read the Twelve Step promises that are found in the Big Book, went to the meeting—and now an incredible feeling of "infinite power and love," like I had read about in the Big Book, was embracing me.

I describe it as a feeling, but it might be more accurate to say it *caused* feelings. Because it wasn't *from* me; that is, I wasn't its source. It was from a Presence visiting me.

As I drove, that Presence grew. As I pulled into my driveway, it settled like a gentle cloud around me. As I went into my house, it went with me. It was the most beautiful experience of my life. It lasted for about an hour, then drifted away.

Every morning I tell God how grateful I am that he gave me this Gift. I know I will never be able to doubt his reality again.

Nicole

"Dad, I want you to know that I'm going to continue to have a relationship with Nicole," my daughter Ally told me when she came home from college that summer. "I'm not asking permission. I'm going to do it. I'm going to stay in touch."

Later she said to me, "I'm going to dinner tonight with Nicole," and asked if I could take her to a local Starbucks where Nicole would meet her and drive from there. Nicole was still too traumatized to come by the house.

I drove Ally up to the Starbucks, and got out and walked across the parking lot with her to Nicole's vehicle. Nicole rolled down her window but stayed behind the steering wheel.

"You look great," I told her.

She looked at me, and this was the first time we had made eye contact since my release from the Retreat, but she had no words for me.

I made one last feeble attempt to reach her. "You know, I think you would really like this version of me," I said.

There was only pain in her eyes. I could see she just wanted to get Ally in the car and get out of there.

I walked back to my car, got in, and started driving home. This was the moment I reached the conclusion that Nicole was not coming back. It hurt, but I saw that if I really loved Nicole, I had to let her go and be free to create her own life and be happy. *I want that for her,* I prayed. *And I ask you to help her find it.* That sincere prayer, in that painful moment, was probably the best evidence of God's work in my life, of my transformation. I would never have considered it before.

But the odd thing was—or perhaps not so odd, the more I've learned about God—*after* I had truly relinquished Nicole to God's will and care, he began to lead her back to me!

It turns out that awkward encounter in the Starbucks parking lot was a revelation to Nicole. She's an extraordinarily intuitive person, and she could sense that something about me had changed. We had a couple of other very small interactions after that. Once she came by the house to pick up some books she'd left behind (the fact that she was willing to come by should have been a clue that something was going on inside her). Another time she stopped by to exchange some photos. Her conviction about my change grew.

I would learn later that she had by this time begun to date again, but only casually. When she went to put on her makeup to prepare for a date, she would end up thinking about me and crying her mascara right off. She was confused, knowing the pain I had put her through yet sensing I was so very different. In the midst of this turmoil, she reached out to a counselor she and I had seen together about our marriage.

"Even in those days, when you were struggling with Joe's drinking," the counselor said to her, "it was obvious the two of you were deeply in love. Who knows? Maybe he has changed and you two are meant to be together again forever. How will you know if you don't connect with him and tell him how you feel and see how he feels? It will take some courage to put yourself out there like that. If you do it, let me know how it goes."

Of course, I didn't know about any of this, so I was surprised when Nicole called me and said, "Can I come over?"

"Sure," I said.

When she arrived, and we stood across from each other in the kitchen, she looked absolutely amazing. And then she started to cry and say, "I just have some unresolved feelings that I want to share with you. I've been thinking so much about you, Joe, and missing you terribly. My heart aches. I still love you."

I didn't know what to say. It meant so much to hear those words from her, but I hadn't heard *the* words I was waiting for: that she wanted us to be together again.

My female readers might slap the page and say, "Oh, you idiot!" But that's what I was waiting for.

Misreading my hesitancy, she said, "Are you seeing someone?"

Like I said, she's very intuitive, and I had to answer, "Yes."

That was like a stab in her heart, and I felt terrible. She started to back away. "Okay, I get it. I just wanted to let you know how I feel and…. I better go."

I followed her out to her car. She stopped before she opened her door, and we stood there staring at each other. It was an electric moment, as if in the whole world only the two of us existed, so intently did we look in each other's eyes. Somehow she pulled her gaze away, got in her car, and drove off.

I did start to wonder: Could she really be interested in me again? Was she really open to coming back together? On the other hand, she was clearly vulnerable at that point, and I didn't want to take advantage of her.

It was a week or so later when I did reach out to her, and it was probably in the most unromantic way imaginable. I called her up and asked, "Hey, would you like me to handle your investments?" I had joined the new investment firm and was actively building my clients, and Nicole came to mind. I knew she trusted me completely as far as money was concerned, and for years I had managed our money together, and I knew all about her needs. So I wondered if she might feel good about me shepherding her accounts again.

"Yes, I would like that," she said.

That led to appointments between the two of us in my office: looking over her account statements, explaining her options, signing paperwork. By that time, there was no doubt about the spark that was flaming between us again.

"It's getting late," I said after she finished signing the papers. "Do you want to go to the restaurant next door and have dinner?"

"Okay."

I don't remember a bite of the meal because I was too busy drowning myself in the renewed love I saw in her eyes.

Afterward in the parking lot, we kissed—just like another *first* kiss—and it was wonderful.

"Are we really doing this?" I asked. "Are we really getting back together?"

"Yes, we are."

I had one question for her: "Nicole, are you sure I've changed, or will you be worried every day that I'll start drinking again? I don't want to do that to you. No one should have to live like that."

"Joe, I have total confidence in you. You're a new person. You're present—attentive—when I talk to you. You're completely honest. You're open about your feelings. The worry that you'll drink again hasn't crossed my mind since that night in the Starbucks parking lot."

And on March 12, 2022, we were married—once again! It was a small ceremony on the sands of Jupiter Beach. We hope to marry *one more time* as well, this time in the Catholic Church, if my appeal for the nullification of my first marriage is approved.

Since day one, our new marriage has been one of those "more beautiful than ever" blessings, but it became even more intimate and close when Nicole—all on her own, no prodding from me—turned to me during Mass one day and, with Holy Spirit-inspired tears in her eyes, said, "I want to be baptized. I want to be Catholic."

That Easter season she was not only baptized but confirmed, and I was her sponsor.

The physical and emotional oneness between any husband and wife is an awesome thing. When you add a spiritual component to it—put God at the heart of it— it's off the charts! That's the oneness Nicole and I now enjoy.

Nicole's return to me is another blessing I can't take credit for. It's all the result of her courage and another dose of God's "infinite power and love."

A Blessing beyond Blessings

When I joined the Knights of Columbus, an online ceremony, called an exemplification, was part of the process. One of the Knights of Columbus officials, Scott O'Connor, noticed my name in the corner of the Zoom screen and said, "Joe, welcome to the Knights, but I have to ask you—are you related to Father Michael McGivney?"

"I am," I said.

(In the spirit of full disclosure, let me say again here that I can't be 100% sure I'm a blood relative of Father McGivney. My first cousin, Dorothea Pacini, has done extensive research into the family tree, including a trip to Kilnaleck, County Cavan, Ireland, where my great-grandfather, Andrew McGivney, was born. She concluded that that same Andrew was likely a second cousin of Father McGivney. My McGivney relatives and Father Michael's McGivney relatives had lived in very close proximity to each other in Ireland, and there is a very high probability that we are indeed related. But complete certainty is impossible, because many birth and baptismal records were burned or destroyed in the Irish War of Independence.)

"That's amazing," Scott said. "Would you be willing to do an interview for our Florida website?"

"Sure."

After that interview appeared, *Columbia Magazine*, the Knights' monthly magazine, called for an interview.

The magazine originally intended a light, sidebar article, because not only had I joined but my son Colin had joined as well. But as the writer, Cecilia Hadley, learned more about me—my sudden healing, my recovery from alcoholism—she said, "Joe, there's a lot more to your story than just your relation to Father McGivney, isn't there?"

"Yes, a lot more."

"Will you share it with me?"

I did, and that interview became a feature story in *Columbia Magazine's* March 2022 edition, mailed out to 1.6 million Knights. The article's title: "A Blessing Beyond Blessings."

I was then invited to be the keynote speaker at the next Knights of Columbus Florida State Convention. It would take place at the Hyatt Regency in Orlando in May of 2022. It was a great privilege. I would be speaking at a black-tie dinner with about 400 Knights and their wives in attendance.

As the convention drew near, and I was continuing to learn as much about Father McGivney as I could before my speech, it suddenly dawned on me: *I need to go to New Haven and see his church in person.* Nicole wanted to go with me, and so we flew up to Connecticut.

Brian Caulfield himself (the Vice Postulator for Father McGivney's sainthood Cause for Canonization) picked us up at the airport in Hartford and drove us to New Haven, where the Knights' impressive 23-story headquarters "Tower" is located. We met some officials, attended Mass, then drove to St. Mary's Church.

It's hard to describe my excitement at being there.

75

St. Mary's is still a fully functioning church, and is the seat of what is now the citywide "Blessed Michael McGivney Parish," with eight churches under its umbrella. It is also the final resting place of Father McGivney, his remains having been moved from the family burial plot in Waterbury, Connecticut, to a sarcophagus inside the church as a part of the canonization process. It meant so much to me to be able to pray over his resting place.

But the most memorable part of our journey took place during a private tour of the Blessed Michael McGivney Pilgrimage Center, which we visited next. The Center's Peter Sonski conducted our tour. He showed us where Father McGivney's relics are kept, including first class relics, such as a few of his bone fragments and locks of his hair, and second class relics, such as the cassock he was originally buried in. Interestingly, though Father McGivney's remains were exhumed over 100 years after his death, the cassock was not degraded and there was still a full head of hair. As I leaned over the glass case displaying these items to the public, I believe I felt Father McGivney right there with me. I must have had a visible reaction because Nicole turned and looked closely at me.

Our trip also included a "McGivney Immersion" tour, again conducted by Peter Sonski. We visited Waterbury, Connecticut, Father Michael's birthplace. We also visited the McGivney family burial plot where Father Michael was originally laid to rest with his family. Our last stop was Saint Thomas parish in Thomaston, Connecticut. Father Michael was the pastor at Saint Thomas when he passed away. Later that day, we returned to Florida. During our flight home, I couldn't stop thinking about Brian Caulfield and Peter Sonski. The time that I spent with them had left a mark on me. Their selfless devotion to Father Michael both moved and inspired me to become a better man, and a better Catholic. I'm so grateful to have met these wonderful men.

That trip fortified me spiritually for my speech at the convention. I had asked Scott O'Connor, the State Deputy of the Knights of Columbus, "How much of my story do you want me to share?"

"No limitations," he said. "Just tell us your story."

So that's what I did, sharing the same story I've told in this book. As I got up to speak, I prayed, *Lord, please let your words flow through me*, just like I pray every time before I tell my story. I spoke for 35 or 40 minutes, baring my soul, explaining what God had done for me. The response was warm and gracious, a standing ovation. But I knew it was God they were applauding.

Afterward, people came up to take pictures with us, or to thank me, or to say, "God bless you, Joe. I'm in recovery too." The last person, waiting patiently and quietly in line to take his picture with us, was a Catholic priest, the chaplain for the State Knights of Columbus Council.

What an honor that night was! If you had told me two years earlier that I would be standing up in front of 800 devout Catholics telling my story, I would have assumed *you* were the one who had been locked up in a psych ward, not me. But as the angel Gabriel said to Mary when he announced she would be the mother of our Lord, "Nothing is impossible with God."

By Grace

I can take no credit for any of the blessings I've related in this book. They are all God's doing. If my life story had been left up to me alone, I'd still be lost in a Wet Brain nightmare in some institution. All of the wonderful things that have happened to me have been by grace, that is, by a gift of God's love.

I have often asked, *God, why did you save me? Me of all people?* I have come to believe he had three purposes:

First, so that through hearing my story others may experience his grace too. The Bible says that "God shows no partiality" (Romans 2:11). If he worked in my life, he will work in yours too. Not in exactly the same way; after all, he's the God who makes no two snowflakes and no two fingerprints alike. His work in your life will be different, but it will be exactly what you need.

Second, so that through hearing my story others might recover from alcoholism and addiction. It is true that some aspects of my story are unique, but recovery from alcoholism and addiction through the power of God and the Twelve Steps is not! Multitudes of people have experienced the same healing. I want you to know that you, or your loved one, can too.

Third, so that through my story others may become aware of Father McGivney and his Cause for Canonization, and that they also will learn that he has proven to be a powerful intercessor. For I believe it was through his intercession in Heaven for me, in response to my Aunt Gerry's prayer, that God chose to reach down and miraculously, suddenly, and completely heal me. To God alone be the glory.

"Don't be afraid. I have redeemed you. I have called you by your name. You are mine." – Isaiah 43:11

Now these three will last: faith, hope, and love. But the greatest of these is love. – 1 Corinthians 13:13

About the Author

Joe McGivney is a devoted husband to his wife Nicole, a proud father to his adult children Ally and Colin, a recovered alcoholic, and a child of God. He currently serves as the Deputy Grand Knight for Santa Maria Council 4999 and is an active parishioner at St. Patrick Catholic Church in Palm Beach Gardens, Florida. Joe is an author and frequent guest speaker at alcohol and addiction treatment centers, correctional facilities, Knights of Columbus events, and parish gatherings. Professionally, Joe is a Financial Advisor with over 30 years of industry experience. In his leisure time, Joe and his wife Nicole love to travel and spend time with family and friends.

Contact Joe at joemcgivney.com

Selected YouTube videos featuring Joe: https://youtu.be/S42pTJntauk — Knights of Columbus Profile. Healing through our Founder's intercession (4:17 minutes)

https://youtu.be/QnB7uotHGAM — Knights of
Columbus. McGivney Miracle (8:57 minutes)

https://youtu.be/Q2cgsyYBFe4 — Catholic RE.CON.
Eddie Trask Interview (51:32 minutes)

https://youtu.be/qvKAUfnBac0?si=fZQcfowTkiAgE5n
y — Blessed Michael McGivney Pilgrimage Center
(59:30 minutes)

The A.A. Promises

1. If we are painstaking about this phase of our development, we will be amazed before we are halfway through.
2. We are going to know a new freedom and a new happiness.
3. We will not regret the past nor wish to shut the door on it.
4. We will comprehend the word serenity and we will know peace.
5. No matter how far down the scale we have gone, we will see how our experience can benefit others.
6. That feeling of uselessness and self-pity will disappear.
7. We will lose interest in selfish things and gain interest in our fellows.
8. Self-seeking will slip away.
9. Our whole attitude and outlook upon life will change.
10. Fear of people and of economic insecurity will leave us.
11. We will intuitively know how to handle situations which used to baffle us.
12. We will suddenly realize that God is doing for us what we could not do for ourselves.

Are these extravagant promises? We think not. They are being fulfilled among us, sometimes quickly, sometimes slowly. They will always materialize if we work for them.

How It Works

Rarely have we seen a person fail who has thoroughly followed our path. Those who do not recover are people who cannot or will not completely give themselves to this simple program, usually men and women who are constitutionally incapable of being honest with themselves. There are such unfortunates. They are not at fault; they seem to have been born that way. They are naturally incapable of grasping and developing a manner of living which demands rigorous honesty. Their chances are less than average. There are those, too, who suffer from grave emotional and mental disorders, but many of them do recover if they have the capacity to be honest.

Our stories disclose in a general way what we used to be like, what happened, and what we are like now. If you have decided you want what we have and are willing to go to any length to get it — then you are ready to take certain steps.

At some of these we balked. We thought we could find an easier, softer way. But we could not. With all the earnestness at our command, we beg of you to be fearless and thorough from the very start. Some of us have tried to hold on to our old ideas and the result was nil until we let go absolutely.

Remember that we deal with alcohol — cunning, baffling, powerful! Without help it is too much for us. But there is One who has all power — that One is God. May you find Him now!

Half measures availed us nothing. We stood at the turning point. We asked His protection and care with complete abandon.

Here are the steps we took, which are suggested as a program of recovery:

1. We admitted we were powerless over alcohol — that our lives had become unmanageable.

2. Came to believe that a Power greater than ourselves could restore us to sanity.

3. Made a decision to turn our will and our lives over to the care of God as we understood Him.

4. Made a searching and fearless moral inventory of ourselves.

5. Admitted to God, to ourselves, and to another human being the exact nature of our wrongs.

6. Were entirely ready to have God remove all these defects of character.

7. Humbly asked Him to remove our shortcomings.

8. Made a list of all persons we had harmed, and became willing to make amends to them all.

9. Made direct amends to such people wherever possible, except when to do so would injure them or others.

10. Continued to take personal inventory and when we were wrong promptly admitted it.

11. Sought through prayer and meditation to improve our conscious contact with God as we understood

Him, praying only for knowledge of His will for us and the power to carry that out.

12. Having had a spiritual awakening as the result of these steps, we tried to carry this message to alcoholics, and to practice these principles in all our affairs.

Many of us exclaimed, "What an order! I can't go through with it." Do not be discouraged. No one among us has been able to maintain anything like perfect adherence to these principles. We are not saints. The point is, that we are willing to grow along spiritual lines. The principles we have set down are guides to progress. We claim spiritual progress rather than spiritual perfection.

Our description of the alcoholic, the chapter to the agnostic, and our personal adventures before and after make clear three pertinent ideas:

(a) That we were alcoholic and could not manage our own lives.

(b) That probably no human power could have relieved our alcoholism.

(c) That God could and would if He were sought.

Source: Reprinted from pages 58-60 in the book Alcoholics Anonymous. Copyright © by Alcoholics Anonymous World Services, Inc. 1939, 1955, 1976, 2001. www.aa.org

Father McGivney

Prayer for the Canonization of Blessed Michael McGivney, Founder of the Knights of Columbus.

God, our Father, protector of the poor and defender of the widow and orphan, you called your priest, Blessed Michael McGivney, to be an apostle of Christian family life and to lead the young to the generous service of their neighbor. Through the example of his life and virtue, may we follow your Son, Jesus Christ, more closely, fulfilling his commandment of charity and building up his Body which is the Church. Let the inspiration of your servant prompt us to greater confidence in your love so that we may continue his work of caring for the needy and the outcast. We humbly ask that you glorify Blessed Michael McGivney on earth according to the design of your holy will. Through his intercession, grant the favor I now present (here make your request). Through Christ our Lord. Amen.

Please report all favors received to:
www.fathermcgivney.org

Painting by Chas Fagan © Knights of Columbus

The SURRENDER PRAYER

God, my Father, I thank you for all that you are, and all that you do for me through your son Jesus Christ. I praise you for my life, for your mercy and for your Eucharist. In Jesus' name, Father, I place myself entirely in your Heart. I surrender to you my whole self, my heart, my mind, my memory, my imagination, my will, my emotions, my passions, my body, my sexuality, my desire for human approval, my weaknesses, my desires, my sins.

I surrender every person in my life to you. I surrender every situation in my life to you. I surrender every relationship I am in to you. I surrender every concern I have to you. I surrender every fear I have to you. I surrender every doubt I have to you. I surrender all confusion I have to you. I surrender all sadness I am experiencing in my heart to you. I surrender all my wounds to you. I surrender all anxiety and worry I have to you. I surrender all that deceives me in my heart to you. I trust you to care for me and others in a perfectly loving way.

As I have emptied myself, and surrendered everything to you, I ask you now, Father, to fill me with your Holy Spirit and all the gifts and fruits of your Spirit. Holy Spirit, you are the source of love, hope, joy, peace, patience, goodness, gentleness, tenderness, faithfulness, humility, and self-control. Purify my desires. Help me to open my heart to you. Help me to become perfectly receptive as a pure child. Help me to believe in your love for me. Help me to hope in your love. Help me to receive from the Most Sacred Heart of Jesus all grace and virtues necessary for me to become

*the person you created me to be. I ask this in the Name
of Jesus Christ, Your Son, God Almighty Father.*

*O Most Holy Immaculate Virgin Mary. I entrust this
prayer to your Heart, and ask you to press it to your
wounded heart and intercede for me to your Son Jesus.
Please help me to be as you are, a perfect disciple, an
obedient servant, a true child of God. Amen.*

Additional Resources

Father McGivney Guild – Join the Guild, membership is free! Submit Prayer intentions, report Favors. You will receive a quarterly newsletter with updates and information about the Cause of Blessed Michael McGivney. www.fathermcgivney.org

Knights of Columbus – Join the Knights! Find a local Council. Meet other Catholic men in your area. Help continue Blessed Michael McGivney's work of caring for the needy and the outcast. Serve others through the numerous volunteer ministries of the Knights of Columbus. www.kofc.org

Alcoholics Anonymous www.AA.org

Al-Anon Family Groups—Help and hope for family and friends of alcoholics www.al-anon.org

United States Conference of Catholic Bishops (USCCB) – Sign up to receive an email each morning of the Daily Readings of the Catholic Mass. www.bible.usccb.org

Reading List

Parish Priest: Father Michael McGivney and American Catholicism by Douglas Brinkley and Julie M. Finster

Alcoholics Anonymous (Fourth Edition)

The Big Hustle: A Boston Street Kid's Story of Addiction and Redemption by Jim Wahlberg

The Man Who Mistook His Wife for a Hat: And Other Clinical Tales by Oliver Sacks

The Four Signs of a Dynamic Catholic: How Engaging 1% of Catholics Could Change the World by Matthew Kelly

Rediscover The Saints: Twenty-Five Questions That Will Change Your Life by Matthew Kelly

The Road to Hope: Responding to the Crisis of Addiction by Keaton Douglas with Lindsay Schlegel

The Unfair Advantage: My Story of Conquering the Beast of Addiction by John Robert Eddy

One Knights Journey: Perspective of a Knights of Columbus State Deputy by Scott O'Connor

Confession All: A Humiliating, Tormented Pilgrimage to God's Will by Eddie Trask

A Message to the Reader

IF YOU LIKED MY BOOK, WILL YOU CONSIDER SHARING ITS MESSAGE WITH OTHERS?

- Write a review on Amazon, Goodreads, etc.
- Order a copy for someone who would be challenged or encouraged by it.
- Mention it in a Facebook post, Twitter update, Pinterest pin, etc.
- Invite me to speak to your group, church, or conference—I love to share the story of God's miraculous work in my life.

Reach out to me at joemcgivney.com

Made in United States
Orlando, FL
10 December 2023

40554146R00055